Put Some Good On My Life

BILLIE BUCKLEY

CROSS
BOOKS

CrossBooks™
1663 Liberty Drive
Bloomington, IN 47403
www.crossbooks.com
Phone: 1-866-879-0502

First published by CrossBooks 11/11/2009

ISBN: 978-1-6150-7094-7 (sc)

Library Congress of Control Number: 2009910333

Printed in the United States of America
Bloomington, Indiana

This book is printed on acid-free paper.

Contents

LEAVING A LEGACY THROUGH MY NEWSPAPER COLUMNS

We begin with a question…where would you have looked for me before my life on this earth was over? My final place will be at the Sunrise Baptist Church Cemetery in Petal. Gerald, my husband, gave me this plot as my 49th wedding anniversary present in 2008. Some present! He also took me on a cruise.

You will find other members of my family buried in Laurel and Hattiesburg and Ted, Miss. My mother, Lois Rayner, and my grandmother, Verna Howard, are buried in Laurel. My father, Billy Horace Yelverton, after being killed in World War II, is buried in Ted. My husband's parents, J. C. and Ruby Buckley, are buried in Hattiesburg.

Back to the question … where would you have gone to find me during my life span? Wherever you go, you will always find a pen or pencil in my hand or my fingers on a computer keyboard. I was, am and always will be a writer. I have written a column for the Hattiesburg American newspaper for more than 20 years.

Who have I loved? I have loved Gerald, my Favorite Preacher-Husband, and my two sons. Steve is a football coach and Stan is also a preacher. I must confess I especially love my two daughters-in-law, Jewell and Kristi, who are my heroes because they love my sons. Then there are my grandchildren: the twins, Adam and Neal, and Anna, Slade and Annaleigh. You will read about my love for them and our parents and friends through my selected columns. But, most of all I have loved my Lord, and He has loved me back.

If you have decided to still look for me you must enter many doors … church doors, classroom doors, sporting event doors, fine art doors, and even doors of sorrow and failure. Open the door. Come on in. Sit a spell with me. Then we will stroll through my writing experiences for the Hattiesburg American. Through the years, I have locked no back doors in my writings. What you read is real.

I have gone back through my columns and found 10 recurring themes. Under each one I selected five or six columns to express the lessons I have learned through writing about real living by writing like I talk. I thank Robyn Jackson, my newspaper editor, who for many years has taught me to write tight and never waste a word.

This is my way to leave a legacy for the next generations of our family, friends and readers. I know the only things you can pass on of lasting value are right and rich relationships with your self, your family and friends, and your God. You are invited to join me on my journey.

Taken from columns written for the Hattiesburg American 1986-2008

CHAPTER ONE:
Sharing Secrets

"I HAVE A SECRET TO TELL YOU. I WANT YOU TO TELL EVERYONE YOU KNOW."

As a writer I open up my life for a bridge to connect with my readers. I share secrets about my family, my teaching days, my downer days and my days of reflection and contentment. My past plays a prominent part in who I am today. I begin with these columns. The six secrets I want you to tell your children and your grandchildren are:

1. Real Lessons Learned from Love Letters
2. What Readers' E-mail Taught Me
3. My Top Ten Uncomfortable List
4. Can You Hear the Background Music?
5. Tune into the "Knock, Knocks" of Life
6. Sharing Secrets about Smiles

Lessons Learned from Love Letters

Very soon teachers will be back in the classroom teaching those lessons to match the mandated test for the coming year. Today I want to teach you some lessons learned from personal letters from my father to my mother and me written while he served in World War II. They were written somewhere in France, Italy and Germany. The postmark on the front of the letters begins in December of 1944 and ends on April 1, 1945, four days before he was killed.

Lesson Number One: Pay Your Debts

"Darling, the next time you go home to Ted I want you to pay Uncle Walk that $1.00 I owe him. I owe Mr. Thompson 50 cents. Pay him too. Also give the church at Ted a tithe out of the money I send home. I don't want to owe anyone, and that is all I owe."

Lesson Number Two: Read to Your Child

"Hello, Billie. I love you very much. Make Mama read to you, and when I get home I will read lots to you. I love you. Dad"

Lesson Number Three: Find Humor in the Fox Holes of Life

"I had to laugh at my buddy last night. He was on guard, and I was in the fox hole. I heard an owl holler… you know like they holler back of Mama's house. He jumped down in the hole and whispered, 'I hear a panther coming!' He was so scared. I could not laugh out loud like I did at home, but I just had to smile and tell our buddies."

Lesson Number Four: Live Right

"Darling, it was hard to leave you and Billie and our little home. But I made up my mind long ago I would live right. If it is God's will I'm coming back home and live until He is ready for me to die. So don't worry about me. I'm not afraid over here. Good night."

LESSON NUMBER FIVE: SUN YOUR BEDS

"I'm glad Pete (Mother's brother) sunned our beds for you. I'm sorry I was not there to do it for you."

LESSON NUMBER SIX: BE A GOOD HOUSEKEEPER

"I'm so proud of how you always keep our house clean. I'm glad you have not changed the room for I can picture it like it was when I was home. If I were home now, would you let me leave my things on the floor? I bet not. Ha!"

LESSON NUMBER SEVEN: BE A WRITER OF LETTERS

(This was the last letter written from somewhere in Germany.) "Darling, I got 27 letters last night and 21 were from you. So I had a book to read. It is so good to hear from home. It makes me happy. Hello Billie, I know you are growing for everybody tells me you are a big girl now. Your mother says you sleep with my picture. Don't forget your Dad. He loves you very much."

He died in a fox hole four days later on April 5, 1945. Hopefully, I have learned well the lessons he left in his love letters to my mother. The greatest mandated test is that they live on through me to our sons and then to their sons and daughters. By the way, his name was Billy Horace Yelverton.

I Got Mail

In my last column I shared my father's WWII love letters to my mother before he died somewhere in Germany on April 15, 1945 at the age of 25.

Today I share some of your emails. One reader wrote, "Thank your for your column. As a new mother, it definitely struck a chord. I have set new daily goals for my family because of the story."

Another wrote, "I just finished reading your Saturday column, and it was special to me. Those were poignant memories for you. What a legacy to leave. If we took your dad's advice, we would have a much better world. Thank you for sharing these last letters with us."

A Touched Reader

Later on another email showed up. "Mrs. Buckley, I was moved by the love, wisdom and decency of the man your dad was. Thank you for sharing him with us. This sharing is another way for him to continue to live on."

A Reader Finds Her Place

The final email came about a week later, "Mrs. Buckley, thank you for sharing your father's letters. They have helped me 'find my place' again. In the past whenever I 'lost my place' I would go to my grandma's house. By the end of the visit my perspective would be well again. At times, I did not know I had lost my place until I left. My grandmother would have liked reading your father's letters, also. I felt honesty, unconditional love and humor in all of them. How refreshing that is. Smiling Now…"

Decision Making Time

Back to the writing of this column…I visited cemeteries a few weeks ago with a cousin. In the Myrick community I found where my granddaddy, Robert Howard, was buried. He died when I was very young. I suddenly wanted to know more about this man who would patiently give out my spelling words as a child.

Follow me now. With birthday number 70 looming ahead, I made a decision. My columns for 21 years were written from life experiences. So, knowing I will never be famous (except to my family and a few friends); I want to leave them a written legacy of who I am "in Christ Jesus." I have begun sorting and sampling my columns for this task.

Just maybe, if some of my family or friends lose their place in life this sharing of my life will help them to find their place. Then the legacy would live on … unconditional love, simplicity and humor found in my father's love letters and in my columns about life.

YOU ARE WELCOME TO JOIN ME

Anybody want to join me? You don't have to be a professional writer. But you have to be a lover of your Lord and your family and a few close friends.

P.S. Aug. 2, 2009, we will be married for 50 years. My Favorite Preacher gave me an early present. A cemetery plot at Sunrise Church! It reminded me of the need to speed up this legacy leaving project.

MY TOP TEN UNCOMFORTABLE LIST

They are everywhere … in newspapers, in magazines and in books. Just look for them and you will find one in almost every publication. Their label is "Top 10 List."

I have a Top 10 List today of the things in my life that make me uncomfortable. Here it is in no particular order.

WHY THEY GOT ON MY LIST

They are close places, oysters, tempers, guns, spelling, rudeness, math, new shoes, roller coasters and perfection.

Why include these on the list? Well, math and spelling I'm not good at; oysters I'm allergic to; rudeness and tempers destroy and hurt; new shoes hurt, too; guns and roller coasters are frightening; close places panic me; and perfection is beyond me.

Yet we read in our Bible, "Be ye therefore perfect, even as your Father which is in heaven is perfect." Matthew 5:48 (KJV).

That's one of those Christian standards we want to ignore, isn't it? It's sort of like "Love your enemies. Do good to them that hate you." That's a real "you-got-to-be-kidding."

PERFECT. WHO ME?

Did I hear you say, "You're right. I'm no saint: just an Ordinary Joe or Jane. Listen, I've never done anything perfect. Mess Up is my middle name."

Maybe we can deal with this if we use a three-step plan that works for me when I read my Bible. First, freeze the scripture in its original historical setting. Then unfreeze it or thaw it out to find the main truth embedded there. Finally, absorb it into your present imperfect life. That could also be called "fleshing it out."

Let's try this out with our uncomfortable thought about perfection from Matthew.

LET'S FREEZE IT

When we freeze it in the past we learn Jesus said this to ordinary folks, just like you and me, by the Sea of Galilee. His words came to be known as the Sermon on the Mount. Also, His words were always powerful and these are no exception.

LET'S THAW IT OUT

Now it's time to thaw it out to find the main truth in its historical setting. That's not easy to take this great truth and unfreeze in a Saturday morning column. Hopefully, I won't reduce it or confuse it or make excuses for it.

Here goes. There are really two words in this teaching: Father and perfection. God's favorite word … so I believe … is Father, not perfection. Based on our relationship with God as our Father, we should be like Him.

So, what one word best describes God? Love. That's it. Jesus was saying, "Be complete in our love for Him, for others and for ourselves as God is complete in is love for you."

LET'S FLESH IT OUT

Now we need to absorb it or flesh it out into our present day experiences.

For today it means my love relationship with others won't be stopped by bitterness or hate or indifference.

It is love that knows when to keep silent and when to be filled with patience.

It is love that understands God has wired each of us differently and that is just fine.

It is love that is strong enough to bear all things, quiet enough to hope, merciful enough to forgive and bold enough to hug each other.

Can You Hear the Background Music?

I heard something recently that just stopped me in my tracks. It grabbed my attention and pointed its finger at my heart. I wish I could show it to you. But, I can't. You do know all the really valuable things in life are those which you cannot see.

Walking by the television these words leaped out at me, "It's important to me how you feel." Now when is the last time you heard those words spoken to you? Better still, when was the last time someone else's feelings were important to you?

Lost Your Melody?

Granted we all get to feeling bruised and weak and worthless at times. There is just not harmony in us. Did I hear you say, "You are right, lady, all the melody in my life has leaked out, and no one is aware of it? There is absolutely no music in me. No even a simple tune."

I have found an answer in this dilemma and it has to do with John Wayne. One day I was not so much watching one of his old movies, but listening to it. That's when I figured out it wasn't the guns and horses and tough cowboys making it exciting. Nor was it the train chugging or the dynamite blowing. It was the background music moving up and down the scales, flashing back and forth from one scene to another.

At times, when the horses rumbled it was blaring and loud with the kettle drums building up the pace. During the night, when the rains fell, the background music was soft and gentle with a slight strumming touch. Never was it silent.

Hearing Others' Background Music

I have come to believe every day we act out the scenes of our lives to the background music of our hearts. If your feelings become important to me then I must hear the background music of my own heart first of all. What makes this melody in me, allowing me to be sensitive to your need of laughter and lightness to release the heavy pounding music of stress or sorrow in me?

It is when we come into His presence and abide in Him; when He becomes more and more at home in our hearts. There we can hear Him speak through the scripture and prayer. We learn to sing in His presence in our life. This reduces the timidity and tiredness, making us want to hum our own tunes with Him.

STAY IN TUNE TO GOD'S HEART

Simply put, when He is our guest, we have an ear for the strumming of each other's soul. I think that is what preachers call discernment. That is when we come to discern the mind of God for others and for circumstances in our life and world. It's when we pray, "You choose, Father, and I choose what You choose".

HELP ME FIND A MELODY OF LOVE TO SHARE

Maybe we could pray this prayer today: "Father, make me to hear the background music of Your presence in my life, so that together, we can walk into the disharmony and discord of another's life. Together, may we help them find a simple melody of love?"

In the early hours of the morning it seems as if the whole world is silent. Let me assure you, it is at this time I best hear this melody of love when He says to me, "My child, it is important to Me how you feel."

Could we find one of His children today and by our words or presence demonstrate to them that it is important to us how they feel? I assure you that will grab their attention just as the background music of that old John Wayne movie grabbed mine.

TUNE INTO THE "KNOCK, KNOCKS" OF LIFE

"Knock, knock."
"Who's there?"
"God."
"God who?"
"The God who loves you."

The big question is … what do we do with this God who loves us?
The answer is simple … we love Him back.

LOVING TO LINGER

What is the purpose of this writing? It's to share my daily early morning experiences of simply loving to linger in His presence and loving Him back.

This real love affair began in the 70's when I prayed, "God, be real to me or leave me alone. I know how to walk the walk and talk the talk."

Through that honest prayer, I soon learned to call him "Father."

CUE CARDS FROM THE BIBLE

I also learned how to follow the cue cards held up by the Holy Spirit to make right choices and investments. I knew the cue cards were right on target because they were words from the Bible.

Once the Holy Spirit held up this cue card for me, "… as they came down from the mountain." Mark 9:9 (KJV).

GIVE UP HOMESTEADING

He led me to know that as a follower of Jesus, I was not born to homestead on one mountaintop experience after another. I had to come down even as He did. Why? Hurting folks don't often dwell on mountaintops.

START WITH PUTTING GOOD ON OTHERS' LIVES

So, how can I put some good (God is good) on others' lives if I am aloof from their struggles? By the way, I think putting good on other's lives means to bear fruit … bring God and His children together so the Holy Spirit will have more room to work.

That is my excuse for being put on this earth as a mother, writer and teacher. I love to linger in His presence daily, to be one with His mind and movements. How about you? Have you learned to love lingering in His presence?

Sharing Secrets about Smiles

"There was something about her that just made you smile."

Do you know someone today who makes you smile? I just heard you sigh, "Lady, this is definitely not a smiling world we live in. Come to think of it, my own family is not one that puts a smile on your face. If I'm perfectly honest with you, I don't see a whole lot of smiling going on in my church or in my job either."

You are absolutely correct. So today this column is devoted to making just one person smile as you see yourself, your family or just maybe your God.

We will begin with a few secrets I'm gonna tell you. Now don't tell anyone. You promise?

Secret #1

My grandchildren got dropped off without any breakfast recently. When I asked them what they wanted for breakfast this was on the menu:

"We want a popsicle, fried okra, yogurt or ice cream, cantaloupe and a mixed drink."

Just in case you are wondering what a "mixed drink" is, that's a Sprite-like drink mixed with juice. We laughed and smiled and had fun about our foolish breakfast adventure that day.

I see this as part of their memories when they grow up to be serious adults. Proverbs 13:22 reads, "A good man (woman) leaves an inheritance to his (her) children's children."

I hope when the name BB, "Billie Buckley", comes to their minds they can smile and say, "We had fun at her house. We got to eat fried okra for breakfast" Please don't tell their mothers.

Secret #2

A few weeks ago while driving 600 miles in one long day, I talked "big" to my husband of 42 years. During a pit stop he bought a book about 1,776 people or events to remember when you think about being an American.

Getting back into the car he started reading to me. Ten miles later, I politely asked him to read to himself. Fifteen miles later I told him to close the book. Twenty miles later I announced to my husband, "If you don't stop reading that book to me, I am going to snatch it out of your hand and throw it out this window. Then I will stop this car and let you drive the last 300 miles!"

Please don't tell that to the couples where we will go in October to lead a marriage retreat. I think I will tell them that the key to our staying power is found in Matthew 9:6 (KJV). It reads like this, "What therefore God has joined together, let no man put asunder." If God puts you together He gives you staying power. He did this for on August 2, 1959. Next year will be 50 years on August 2, 2009.

CHAPTER TWO:

Just Being Real ... Period

"LORD, MAKE ME REAL AND NOT RELIGIOUS."

Beginning in the 1970's I prayed, "Father, be real to me or leave me alone. I know how to play this game. I know how to talk the talk and walk the walk. I even know how to dress tacky like a preacher's wife." It was at this point He brought someone into my life who had something I did not have. I wanted what my friend had. The newspaper columns in this chapter open up the real Billie Buckley who seeks to have a real relationship of oneness with her Heavenly Father.

1. Lord, Make Me Real and Not Religious
2. Do You Ever Miss the Point?
3. Forget About Blooming ... Let's Just Survive
4. What Valuables Do You Have in Your Safe?
5. Come Stroll with Me

Lord, Make Me Real and Not Religious

I've got a list. It's not a list of things to do or be. It's a list of things I don't care about. Now I've never been passionate about being fashionable, fantastic or free spirited. How about it? Do you have a list of what you don't want to be? Granted, most folks' dream lists consist of what they aspire to be. Not mine.

Oh, I forgot, there is one more thing on my list. I have never aspired to be religious or spiritual. Those are not my favorite words, and quite frankly, people who act religious or talk spiritual are not on my favorite list either.

For you to get this, maybe we had better back up and let me tell you a story. Once upon a time my Favorite Preacher let me go with him on a big boat ride to the Caribbean. The scene took place on a small private island. The characters were unknown to each other. The conversation began on a friendly yet superficial note. Follow closely and listen in as the retired doctor spoke first to me.

You Decide … Being Real or Religious

"So your husband is a minister. We don't practice religion in our family in a formal way. Let me ask you something personal. Did you become religious before or after you met your husband?"

"Actually, I've never wanted to be religious or spiritual."

"Have I insulted you? I am sorry if I have."

"By no means have you insulted me. Long ago in the front of my Bible I wrote these words: 'Lord, make me real and not religious.'"

A Confusing Conversation

"I don't quite understand."

"It all has to do with relationship…a real relationship with a personal God. Because I am a Christian, I believe this is made possible as I accept His plan to establish this real relationship through His Son, Jesus Christ."

"How can there be a personal God who has the capacity to care about so many individuals? It just doesn't make sense."

CLEAR ANSWER

"I believe this because the Bible tells me so based on events and not just lofty ideas.   C.S. Lewis once wrote Jesus was either who He said He was, or a lunatic or a liar. I had a choice to accept Him or reject Him, but not to ignore Him. Everyone has that choice today."

"I think I understand your reasoning. Is it you have a real faith that works in a real manner because of your faith in God's say-so in your Bible?"

"You got it."

GOD'S SURPRISE

To end this story, let me back up to the beginning of that day when I had read from "The Message" Ephesians 3:17. Paul wrote, "This is my lifework: helping people understand and respond to His love message. It came as a sheer gift to me, a real surprise, God handling all the details."

That morning I asked for the opportunity to help someone understand and respond to His love. He handled the details by giving me the chance in a real conversation with a real person on a real beach to say simply, "The thing is this: My God is real to me. He wants to be real to you, too."

And that, my friend, was God's surprise for me for that particular day. It is true. We serve a God of surprises when we follow the details He has worked out for us to tell others about His love story. I pray every day I won't mess up His story by the way I speak, write or live.

DO YOU EVER MISS THE POINT?

Do you ever feel like you are missing the point? I do. One week when I picked up a magazine it pointed out to me who the Best Dressed and the Worst Dressed folks were in the celebrity world. May I confess something to you? I couldn't tell the difference! You see, at this stage of my life, the point has definitely been missed when it comes to fashions. My criteria are simple. Is it comfortable? How much will it hide?

In relationship to some programs on television I am missing the point, too. Many big to-dos are being made over programs where the dialogue is one-dimensional. Learning the lines must be simple. You just learn one word and use it over and over again. That's the word my mother would have washed my mouth out with soap for using. No. That's not right. She would have surely made me swallow the entire bar of soap!

MY ONE CLAIM TO FAME

Sometimes I wonder from whom folks take their cues. If you have ever performed, you know there are times when you forget and someone has to cue you in. My only "claim to fame" is way back in the 50's. At Mississippi College I got to be the young girl Emily in the drama department's presentation of Thornton Wilder's "Our Town."

In the play Emily has to stand on a ladder most of the time as she remembers. Early in the rehearsals, this Emily (me) stood on a ladder and did the opposite. She did not remember. She forgot. She forgot her lines and had to ask for cued-in help from the one holding the script.

KEEPING IN STEP

As a Christian, I have been reminded recently that maybe I have missed the point, too. You see, our Lord didn't keep in step with the world and its legalistic values. He got His cues from a different source.

This reminder came to me as my Sunday School class and I had begun studying the book of John in the New Testament. From the very first lesson it has been made clear that Jesus never missed the point because He took His cues from His Father. Maybe that's why He went away from the crowd so much to be alone with the Father.

GET YOUR CUES FROM AUTHOR OF SCRIPT

We church-going Christians can miss the point entirely if that's all we do … go to church to find something attractive in the music, in the preacher, in the building or in the crowd. And there we remain, on the same level year after year. We too have to get alone at times, away from the crowd, away from the entertainment. We need to get our cues for a higher level of living beyond that which is only attractive to our ears and eyes and egos.

Am I suggesting we become a Lone Ranger Christian? By no means. My suggestion is very simple. If you only meet Him at church, you may have missed the main point. The point being, He is the Author of the Script. When we forget, His word (the Bible) is there to cue us into His way of thinking, of handling problems, of relating to others in love. His way is not loud. It's not showy. It's not even entertaining at times. It comes to me in the early morning quietness as He cues me in on how to deal with my hurts, my failures and my praying for others.

WHAT HAPPENS WHEN YOU FORGET THE LINES?

One cue He gave me recently was "I will fight for you, and you hold your peace." Hopefully, I won't miss that point, as I desire to move to a new level of relationship with Him and with others. This is where my thoughts and actions are based on cues from the Author of the Word. When I am prone to forget the lines, His Holy Spirit will cue me in. All I have to do is to ask.

Forget About Blooming ... Let's Just Survive!

Once I read in the Saturday paper I was to conduct a seminar with a beauty consultant and a health educator. How did I do that? Better still how do I always get myself into such situations?

Through a previous column, I remember having confessed to the world that we ate gravy on our rice, and that I hated rice cakes. I even went so far as to mention my love for Snicker Bars and Reese's Peanut Butter Cups ... so much for impressing the health educator.

Confession Time

While I am in this confessing mode, if you had asked for a description of me during my 32 years of teaching school, my students would have agreed on these details:

"She's the gray-headed teacher whose hair needs fixing. She probably doesn't have on any lipstick and there is chalk dust all over her skirt. Her nails won't be polished either. Mrs. Buckley never wears high heels, and she won't have a pretty scarf around her neck."

Do you think the beauty consultant was impressed with those credentials? You are getting the drift of this situation, aren't you? They were to talk about blooming, and most of the time I struggled to just survive!

Just What is a Molehill?

To continue with this story, we have to enter the classroom where my students were talking about idioms. "Making mountains out of molehills" was our example of an idiom. At the conclusion of this discussion one bright student waved his hand and asked, "Mrs. Buckley, just what is a molehill?" What would you have told him?

I'm not sure what a molehill is, but I do know about mountains. Today we can be convinced one mountain so many of us erect and face is a lack of self-confidence and a poor self-image. As Christians, we should believe a good self-image is a self in step with God, and a self-confident person lives out the truth of who we are in Christ Jesus.

How to Write Graffiti on God's Name

How does our lack of self-confidence rob God? It writes graffiti all over His name and moves Him out onto the margins of our lives. Why do we sell ourselves short and show disrespect for the abilities He has given us?

Maybe it is because we are afraid or just lazy; maybe we can't bring ourselves to make a decision; maybe we can't take rejection; or maybe we don't have what it takes to keep on keeping on.

Which Self Controls You?

Let's become child-like and use our imaginations to listen in on a conversation between Self-Pity and Self-Respect:

Self-Pity asks, "Why am I taking up space on this earth?"

Self-Respect answers, "I am aware of my own existence on this earth to bear fruit."

Self-Pity whines, "I am hopeless, unworthy of a friend or someone to love me."

Self-Respect announces, "I have God's wisdom to look beyond every hopeless relationship and task."

The main difference is Self-Pity takes endless futile inventories of its own failures while Self-Respect acknowledges its weaknesses, gets up and moves on.

A Happy Ending to This Doom and Gloom Column

Finally, there is a happy ending to this doom and gloom column. When I met the beauty consultant, she had gray hair … just like me. And it gets better. The health educator was going home to eat Fritos … just like me.

Hopefully, you have been encouraged today to start liking yourself and stop making mountains out of molehills. You start by taking your eyes off yourself and keeping your focus on God. It works for me.

What Valuables Do You Have in Your Safe?

Once upon a time my Favorite Preacher and I were in a hotel room with a safe. The instructions read, "Place valuables inside safe and lock by …" I knew right away I had found a column. Here it is.

What valuables would you place in a safe today? Maybe we had better establish this fact: only those things you don't want to lose are valuable. Probably, some of our valuables are priceless even though they didn't cost a penny.

Shared Memories are Valuable

Most everyone values shared memories. Those old scrapbooks with the yellow pages would definitely be classified as a prize. Memories naturally deal with the past. Yet, we must ask, "What about our dreams for the future?" No matter how old you are, I hope you have a dream in your heart, a vision, a goal and a destination to reach. Not only is the past valuable, but the future is worth fighting for. Consider it valuable.

Other Common Valuables

Good health must be put in my safe. I saw a book the other day entitled "The Joy of Aging." I got my first Medicare card a few years ago. Do you suppose that is what the author had in mind?

I surely value my family. In fact, I value them enough to stay behind the curtain until I am needed. Let me confess. I peek out and speak out at times when I should not. I am thankful they are quick to understand and forgive.

Special friends are placed carefully in my safe of valuables. I do not want to lose these folks whom I feel comfortable around; those whom I can trust with my rotten moods and downer days; those who share my victories with personal cheers.

Common Test for Valuables

The church is valuable to me. I know some of you reading this don't hold this same view. How can you tell if something is valuable to you? If you spend time there, then certainly it is important to you. To me, the church building a special place but it is also special because that's where I go to meet God and worship Him with other believers. Then I leave to serve Him. I believe He values this, too.

You have to look in an antique green trunk containing shoe boxes to locate my next valuable. There you will find old love letters written to my mother by my father during World War II. In an abstract way I place liberty and freedom in my chest of valuables. I can think of no other reason for a young father to die at the age of 25 on a field somewhere in Germany. I along with countless others have earned the right so say to politicians, "Don't use this issue of any war to fan the fires of your party's elections. His death is far too valuable to me for you to prostitute it in this manner."

GIVE YOUR VALUABLES AWAY

The world instructs us to protect our treasures. As Christians, Christ instructs us to give them away. His exact words are, "It is more blessed to give than to receive." Empty your safe today. You will be blessed with the greatest valuable: God's smile of approval.

COME STROLL WITH ME

At times my phone will ring. An uneasy voice ventures this question, "Our speaker can't come at the last minute; can you come?"

The question is answered with calmness, "Certainly, I would love to share this fellowship with your group." Now these words can be spoken because I am learning to stroll. In fact I value strolling.

Some of you reading this column are not strollers. You are marathon runners. You are like the Energizer Bunny that goes on and on. I applaud you. I value you in my life. But, at times I just can't keep up with you.

ESPECIALLY FOR NON-STROLLERS

Others are sprinters. You talk fast, move fast and get things done in a hurry and move on to the next undertaking. Again, I applaud you. I value your contribution to our churches and other organizations. Yet, at times I get mixed up when I am around you.

Then there are strollers. You take time to dream and swing. You have time to actually listen to others. Your pace is unhurried, leaving time for an occasional hug. You seem to add a velvety touch to the roughness of life. You are not passive. You are very much alive because opening up to others is easy for strollers. I like strollers. I need strollers in my life.

I want to say thank you for those who have strolled with me through happy and sad days, teaching days and learning days, bad days and good days. Why do I value strolling and strollers?

WHY STROLL?

- Strolling is an antidote to all the foolish endeavors in our lives.

- Strolling can vanquish negative feelings from our mind, renewing our strength and purposes.

- Strolling gives us time to think about the emptiness of our lives and how they need to be filled with Kingdom or true values.

- Strolling keeps us vibrant and full of life. It encourages us to put voice to those true values in a sometimes vulgar world.

WHAT TO TELL OTHERS

Put a voice or feet to your heart right now. Tell someone you value him or her. Take time to stroll with your children, your grandchildren and your spouse. That's a great way to let others know you are thankful for their invasion in your life, no matter how long ago or for how short a time.

I have this on good authority, for last week as I prayed through Ephesians, I discovered this truth in Ephesians 2:10: ("The Message")

"We are God's masterpiece. He has created us anew in Christ Jesus. (We have value.) So we do the good things he planned for us to do long ago."

Do a good thing and say thank you to someone today who has taken time to stroll with you.

CHAPTER THREE

Celebrating Ordinary Days

Are you like me? You would love to soar like an eagle with lofty ideas and celebration. But, you can never get off the ground. The runway is filled with small packages of ordinary living taking up all you time and energy. May I suggest to you there is splendor in the ordinary, and peas and cornbread can have an exotic taste? Let's find out how to celebrate the quiet days of life.

1. The Splendor of the Ordinary
2. You Don't Have to Decorate Everything
3. Celebrating Warm-Hearted Folks
4. Celebration of Freedom at a Cemetery
5. One Ordinary Working Mother's Mail

THE SPLENDOR OF THE ORDINARY

Is your life filled with spectacular special events? Is it glamorous and glowing, exciting and challenging? Do you wake up each day eager to meet the day's blessings and opportunities? Are you surrounded by understanding, supportive people?

Did I hear you laugh? Maybe it was a sob I heard?

Some of you are thinking, "If she only knew--my life is bogged down in routine ruts. It is one big boring demand. Just thinking about Thanksgiving and Christmas celebrations makes me want to sneak away and hide. Ordinary responsibilities leave me with no time or energy to wake up each day with eagerness. It could better be described as tiredness or anxiety."

Me, too. Don't get me wrong--I would love to soar like an eagle with lofty ideas and ideals. But, I can never get off the ground. The runway is filled with small packages of ordinary daily demands on my time and energy.

OPEN UP THOSE SMALL INSIGNIFICANT PACKAGES.

Let's open these small insignificant packages in our lives keeping us from becoming somebody exciting and important. Maybe you can't be known as a great motivating speaker because you spend so much time preparing and teaching small groups about God's Word and how to apply it to their lives.

You say there is no time for you to be part of a swinging social crowd? You're only raising kids to like themselves, get along with their friends and know God personally. You are only providing a good stable home for them ... nothing fancy, just solid.

Did I hear you complain you never get to entertain properly because someone is always dropping by to share an ordinary meal of peas and corn bread? The sign on your table reads, "Welcome" and not "Elegance."

Do you have the "eye of the tiger?"

People who really seem to impress the world have what some call "the eye of the tiger." If that is what it takes for success, then color me failure. There are just too many balls to juggle in my world. No way can I keep my eye on only one as those "eye of the tiger" folks do.

What about the world's standards?

Granted, we get confused about standards. The world's standards are always glamorous. If you don't believe me, pick up a magazine and look at the advertisements. What do you see? Glamorous women advertising color for your eyes that make you an unforgettable woman. Perfume for your neck that releases your splendor, making you as alluring as an emerald. Powder for you face that makes you look flawless. Never worked for me.

So what is the bottom line? What needs to be said to sum up this rambling? It's so simple you may be insulted. We must first have spent a quiet time with our God face-to-face. This is when we are led to say, "You choose, Lord. I choose what you choose." That's a good balance for all of us teetering on the edge. So, if we are keeping our lives balanced with His plumb line (The Bible), then color us successful.

Finding splendor in peas and corn bread.

Yes, there is splendor in the ordinary, and peas and cornbread can have an exotic taste. It's up to you. Taste and see. Then go out to celebrate the ordinary days of your life.

YOU DON'T HAVE TO DECORATE EVERYTHING

First of all, I've got some good news. The good news is, "You don't have to decorate or fix everything." Isn't that great!

If you are not a decorator or fixer by nature, then you cannot imagine the freedom given by those words.

LIVING IN A WORLD WITH A DIRE NEED TO BE FIXED UP

Some of you may argue, "We live in a world in dire need of big-time decorating or fixing up." You are right. Everything and every relationship will get broken or frazzled at one time or another. May I suggest we can become too single-minded? In the bustle of the businesses of life we are in danger of bumping into others with our insensitivity of them.

Two words for all frantic fixers are needed … let go. Lighten up a bit. Let go of trying to fine-tune everybody and everything around you. Let go of trying to make everything just right.

Do your find yourself drawing back from these words or embracing them?

YOU GOT THE MARTHA COMPLEX?

Sometimes our desire to decorate everything hinders our relationship with those around us. The next false step we take is to make them feel uncomfortable by taking on the "Martha Complex." In the Bible, Martha was part of the family whom Jesus loved to visit. One day He dropped by for dinner. Her sister Mary wasn't helping with the meal preparation for Jesus. Understand Mary wasn't into gourmet cooking.

Just like some of us, Martha complained to Jesus, "Don't you care my sister has let me do all the fixing up and all the work by myself?"

MARCHING MARTHA OR MEDITATING MARY

We ask this question, too. The answer is to know that only God-given desires to fix or decorate something or someone will be granted His permission and power. You might be asking, "What are the things

God gives us permission and power to fix up as a Marching Martha or a Meditating Mary?"

I'm not sure. I do know He does ask me to meet the needs of others as I become aware of them. They may need to be appreciated, to be applauded, to be given space, to be understood, to be loved. They might need you or me ... just you or me.

SITTING ON THE CURB AND APPLAUDING

Don't forget to look around and find those who never sat on the curb and booed as we marched by. They just sat there quietly and applauded us with their acceptance. Personally, I'm not much into big-time decorating; but I would love to meet you on the curb and help with the applauding.

CELEBRATING WARM-HEARTED FOLKS

Have you been anywhere lately where these words are spoken: "It's cold in here? I might need to rephrase that question. Have you been around any cold-hearted folks lately?

Where do you find them? Without looking you could find them in your home, in your work place, in your school and even in your churches.

HOW TO FIND A COLD HEART

How do you know a cold heart? There is a simple way you can get your mind around this question. You feel it with your heart. You feel the indifference, the mistrust and the meanness. Their body language and negative facial expressions warn you, "I'm watching. You better be careful. I'm gonna get you!"

But I've got some good news--this world is also filled with warm-hearted folks. If you run into one of these warm hearts, capture it for the lean seasons of your life when you need others to stand in the gap for you.

CATCHING A WARM-HEARTED CREATURE

How do you know you have cornered one? Here are some sure-fire signs. A warm-hearted creature can be caught:

- Smiling and hugging

- Petting a dog and tickling a baby

- Enjoying a bowl of ice cream or a swing

- Reading children's books

They don't keep score or give you a grade. Never do they look for perfection in you, but they always expect you to do your best. They believe in you. Around every corner there they are, taking stock of your achievements and victories and hardly noticing your defeats. Come to think of it, they are not always trying to fix something … namely me or you.

LESSONS LEARNED FROM OTHERS

Warm-hearted folks are teachers. What have they taught me?

- How to relax and doodle during scheduled play times

- How to spontaneously hit a trash can with a piece of wadded up paper

- How to enjoy a ballgame with any shape ball

- How to practice grace … giving others what they need and not what they deserve

GET READY FOR THE GENUINE THING

Do you remember the Golden Rule, "Do unto others as you would have them do unto you?" Matthew 7:12 (KJV) Could we paraphrase that to mean, "Figure out what you need and grab the initiative and do for others what you want them to do for you." That's definitely a warm-hearted move.

These warm-hearted folks are also smart because pat answers or pat formulas are not part of their make-up. This allows them to sit down and cry with you; yet, they don't come apart easily. I find myself comfortable in their presence. As a writer, my hope is you are comfortable reading this column.

Due to their warm-hearted condition they sparkle, they marvel a lot--they dare to be the genuine thing.   My point is simple. Warm-hearted folks are a delight to be around. Others can take delight in them and so can God. Can you get your mind and heart around those words?

DO YOU KNOW GOD'S FAVORITE NUMBER?

As a Christian can our Lord take delight in us today? If he can then others can, too. You can't separate the two. By the way, you do know God's favorite number, don't you? I have been meaning to tell you. It is ONE. Remember Jesus praying for us to be one with Him even as He and The Father were one? When you are one with His mind and His heart nothing can separate you from being a warm-hearted believer. I find these words are easy for me to get my mind and my heart around. Hopefully, you have had the same feeling. Be good. Be smart. Be warm-hearted.

CELEBRATING FREEDOM AT A CEMETERY

"Billie, I love you very much. Have your teeth come out yet? I would like to see you with them out. In another day or two you will have a birthday. I wish I could be there to help you eat your dinner. Be sure to have a cake and candles and remember me when you blow them out."

My father wrote this letter from somewhere in Germany in early 1945 to his five-year-old daughter. He never got to see me with my baby teeth out, learning to ride a bike, being silly or scared. He never got to see my wedding dress, my babies or my grandchildren. He was killed April 5, 1945 while spearheading a large-scale attack on a German stronghold in Western Germany.

A CEMETERY BIRTHDAY CELEBRATION

Let's fast-forward our story. The location is a small community called Ted near Louin, Mississippi. Smack-dab in the middle of Ted is a rare thing … a quaint white church with a small well-kept cemetery. This was the setting for our birthday party celebration where we blew out candles and remembered our father, our grandfather and our great-grandfather, Billy Horace Yelverton.

My husband, sons, daughters-in-law and grandchildren went with me to celebrate his life. I wish you could have been there. First of all, you would have to be part of the preparation for the party. With my grandchildren in tow, we bought our cake and flowers. Can't leave out the bubbles to blow and the quilt my mother made to sit and roll on under the shade of the trees.

You need to listen to my story told to Annaleigh, Slade, Anna, Adam and Neal. This story was shared on the way to the party celebration in the cemetery.

A SIMPLE CONVERSATION WITH MY GRANDCHILDREN

"He loved to play basketball. People have told me he was so good. He was real smart too. I know he loved this church we are going to, his family and his country. This Purple Heart reminds us of how brave he was."

THE GREAT GIFT OF MEMORY

This was not a memorial service that took place. This was a birthday party to celebrate a gift of memory to my grandchildren. You see, they got to go to the church he helped to keep alive, choose their own flowers to scatter on his grave, carry the flag that was on his casket, sing, run and play with bubbles.

If you were there, you would have heard this loud singing and laughter and quiet prayers by my husband and son. You could have blown out the birthday candles and held one as you remembered his life. I take away one memory from our celebration.

Caught up in the moment, one of our grandsons said to me, "BB, I want to be just like your father when I grow up!"

REMEMBER THEIR GIFT OF FREEDOM

So, on days of celebration for our freedom and country, could we put aside our differences and together run and play, carry flowers, blow bubbles, wave the flag, and remember all our fathers who gave their lives to make possible this celebration of freedom?

P.S. If you can go to my website www.billiebuckley.com you will find this story and pictures to go with it. If you are reading this somewhere around the year 2009, it's safe to assume it is still there. If it is a much later time, don't bother.

ONE ORDINARY WORKING MOTHER'S MAIL

This ordinary letter was written many years ago to one working mother from a now grown-up child. I share it to encourage mothers who work outside the home and to enlighten folks who have recently questioned the wisdom of doing so.

"Dear Mother, as I look back on my growing up years I realized you juggled two great responsibilities. You were not only a homemaker but had a full time job. I remember all the times you made it look so easy. Yet, I never remember you telling me you couldn't help me or take time for me because of being tired or stressed out. You never yelled at us because of your work or took out your frustrations on our family. (Okay, maybe there were a few times.) **That was my home with a working mother.**

"I always felt our home was a place I could be comfortable and relaxed around people who cared for me and my sometimes obnoxious friends. They were welcome to come and drink incredible amounts of Kool-Aid, play endless games of basketball, eat any meal with us, watch television or just relax. **That was my home with a working mother.**

"Thank you for being active in our church. Your couples' class was something else. Who else could get most of the local football staff to come to Sunday School? You helped instill in me the importance of the Bible, the church and a relationship with God. You shared your values with me without trying to force them on me. Without that, I would be lost today. **That was my home with a working mother.**

"Thank you for praying for me. One of my treasures is the little green book of prayers you wrote in each day for me as you included God in our everyday lives. Even today I know in a world of uncertainty, my mother still prays for me. **That was my home with a working mother.**

"You encouraged me to do my best in school and in sports. You loved me the same… in defeat or in victory. That is the key. I never doubted your unconditional love. I always knew I could come home to a place where I would be hugged. **That was my home with a working mother. Thank you for being living proof that a working mother can be a real mother."**

This personal letter was shared to make a simple statement to all working mothers. **Hang in there.** Though you are not home all the time, you can raise kids with God's help, who, when they are grown, have good memories. Best of all, they still look forward to coming home. I'm thankful the grown son who wrote this letter still likes to walk in our back door.

CHAPTER FOUR:

Meandering Through Marriage and Other Relationships

Do you know God's favorite word and His favorite number?

I write about relationship because I happen to believe that is God's favorite word. Why else would He send His son to die on a cross except to establish a relationship with His children? What is His favorite number? One. Jesus prayed that we might be one even as He was one with His Father. I think that is called discerning the mind of God.

May I add this thought? Not only is that being one with His mind, but one with His motive of love and His movements. I have come to understand He desires for us to have right relationship with others, with ourselves and with Him as our Father. That is why I write … to put some good on others' lives. Remember, God is good. So if we put good on their lives we are actually putting God's goodness on them. I wrote these columns about relationships.

1. Restoring Your Sinking Marriage
2. Hello, Young Lovers
3. Healthy Mother-in-law Relationships
4. Strange Ways to Learn About Relationships
5. The Most Important Relationship of Your Lifetime

RESTORING YOUR SINKING MARRIAGE

Although I've sung "How Great Thou Art" for many years, it was as though I had heard the words for the very first time. "…when I in awesome wonder, consider all the worlds Thy hands hath made."

Do you hear it, too? Let me put it this way. When was the last time you considered anything in awesome wonder?

Most of the time we look at our jobs, our houses, our relationships with our children or our spouses and never consider it to be an awesome wonder … just an awesome confusing mess!

IS YOUR MARRIAGE A CONFUSING MESS?

Admit it; life does get to be confusing at times, doesn't it?

You are told from early childhood to work hard and you will be justly rewarded. Then one day you look around and the material rewards have passed you by. It's not hard work, but a piece of paper or who you know that is the standard for your making a living. Years of experience, plus know-how coming from trial and error, just don't count.

That is an awesome, confusing situation to deal with. If you aren't careful it can surely rob you of your sense of wonder!

That baby, who can fill you with such wonder and joy, can grow up and break your heart, filling you with a sense of deep sorrow.

The greatest loss of wonder comes between a man and woman in marriage. My favorite preacher and I fight a lot. We fight together to keep a sense of wonder in our marriage. Now, we lose some battles every once in a while, but we have never lost the war.

What's our secret? I'm not sure he wants this told, but if you promise not to tell … my husband and I always try to do the following:

… Try to fuss over each other.

… Remember to laugh and keep a good sense of humor.

… Forget to nag each other.

… Brag on each other's appearance and effort.

… Permit no one to know we may be going through a "dry spell."

… Never speak these words: "None of your business."

... Agree in front of our sons, and allow no one to criticize the other in front of us.

... Learn to say, "I'm sorry."

...Act as if we are each other's partner and not each other's property.

... Acknowledge each other's tiredness and hard work without expecting Superman or Superwoman to emerge at the end of a busy day.

... Strive to keep our home holy with God's presence for the joys of growing old together.

This so our children can "rise up and call us blessed." (Hopefully, they will just always call!)

DON'T LEAVE OUT THE MAIN INGREDIENT

Oh, my, I've left out the main ingredient. What I left out is kin to making a strawberry pie and leaving out the strawberries.

It's just a short four-letter word. When you put the letters together, they spell TIME.

If you want to keep the sense of wonder in your marriage, then take the time to let your wife or husband know that you still look at them in awesome wonder, considering all the good and happy times in your life together.

DID I HEAR YOU SIGH?

Did I hear you sigh? Are you thinking, "But we have wasted so many days with coldness in our heart. You can't imagine how barren our marriage is!"

I just read from Joel 2:25 (NKJV), "And I will restore to you the years that the locust hath eaten." I don't know what has eaten away at your marriage, but God is still in the restoring business.

A Wedding Letter to Our Son

Many years ago I needed to write my weekly column, but instead I found myself writing a letter to our No. 2 Son who was to be married in a few days.

Maybe it was right for me to share these thoughts on his wedding day in hopes they would express the feelings of young lovers. Maybe it was right to encourage those who may have lost their first love to look for it and recapture it.

What Does Love Look Like?

Now you may be thinking, "But you don't understand. It's been so long that I have completely forgotten what love looks like."

Let me help you in your search through the letter I wrote to my son sixteen years ago.

"Today, July 15, 1989, is your wedding day. Thirty years ago I married your father. (Let us update this to 49 years ago.) During these years we have come to know what committed love really is and exactly how it feels and what it looks like.

A Picture of Young Love

"Today, my son, your love is young and strong, and you know perfectly well how it looks. Nevertheless, through the years and tears, you may lose sight of it. Whenever you do, I hope this letter will be a gentle reminder.

"What does love really look like? It has many faces and moods.

"It is candlelight softness right now. But, one day, it may have to become hard and tough. You may still call it love.

A Picture of Committed Love

"On this, your wedding day, your love is courageous and determined. Know that one day it may be fearful and weak. You may still call it love.

"Optimism and enthusiasm can be seen in your love painting today. One day despair and hopelessness may splash across the canvas. You may still call it love.

"After your wedding march can't be heard or even remembered, committed love takes over.

"Today love is beautiful and elegant. Yet, there will come days when it becomes plain and homely from work and stress. You may still call it love.

"Remember this ... one thing committed love doesn't do is keep score; and it never throws in the towel. It may want to, but it can't. Why? Because of an old-fashioned commitment made many years ago.

"As you are know, you can legally get out of anything – from taking a life to destroying a relationship. You are making a love commitment today. May it last forever 'till death do you part.

When She is Lost, Be Her Light

"Please remember this also:
When she is scared, be her strength.
When she is sad, be her joy.
When she is tired, be her energy.
When she is lonely, be her friend.
When she is happy, be her laughter.
When she is lost, be her light.
When she is proud, be her applauding audience.
When she is playful, be her playmate.
When she is a mother, be her helpmate."

Healthy Mother-in-law Relationships

Letter to My Daughters-in-Law

I must admit to you that I still get nervous about being a new mother-in-law. Reading Ann Landers lately hasn't helped either, nor does it help that all the bad mother-in-law jokes involve mothers who have sons and not daughters. That means I could mess up twice!

Maybe we need to start with a new set of Ten Commandments. From Moses to this day they have been given.

A Mother-in-law's Ten Commandments:

- *Thou shalt make thy daughter-in-law special.*

- *Thou shalt be supportive.*

- *Thou shalt ask no questions.*

- *Thou shalt plan the right amount of love.*

- *Thou shalt limit thyself.*

- *Thou shalt avoid advice.*

- *Thou shalt not be overly sensitive.*

- *Thou shalt not be too talkative.*

- *Thou shalt not be domineering.*

- *Thou shalt keep thy arms open and thy mouth closed.*

Now, will you allow me to use this column to express a mother-in-law's heart through an open letter to all our daughters-in-law?

Dear Daughters-in-Law

"Those are strange words to me. I never had a daughter so this relationship may be lacking in refinement.

"To begin with, always know that when there is turmoil in your life, I hope I can reflect the calmness you need.

"When there is perplexity and uncertainty, I want you to know that you can count on me to be sure and unquestioning.

HOLD ON TIGHT

"Hold on tightly. Hold on even when that is all you can do. Hold on to your dreams, to your laughter, and most of all, hold on to my son - even if you have to shake him a time or two while you are holding on.

"At times, all you will be able to do is to survive. You will find that it's hard to survive in our mostly:

Madonna World with an apron tied around your waist and a child on each hip.

Computer World when all you know how to use is a pencil.

Aerobics World when you are too tired to move.

Winners World when you strike out every time you get up to bat.

Stylish World when all your labels read TACKY.

Fast Lane World when you have run out of gas.

YOU CAN FIND ME OFFSTAGE IN THE WINGS

"Please know that if you need me in any of these worlds I'll be offstage in the wings. My role is not up front or on center stage in the lives of my sons. I gladly have given up that part and enjoy the stand-by role. I now have time for a starring role in the life of their father.

KEEP ON KEEPING ON

"Remember those words of encouragement, Hold on. Let me share with you the next step.

"Keep moving. Keep moving in your own lane of growth and confidence; yet never knock down those around you as you move forward.

"Finally, dig deeper - deeper in the love you now feel for my son, in your personal faith, in your mothering moments, in your daily decision-making, and in your times of crisis.

Nobody is Suppose to Like a Mother-in-Law

"Everybody knows that you are not 's'pose to' like your mother-in-law! I hope you and I can change that 's'pose to.' I have an idea we can do this because we have at least one thing in common - we both love the same person.

"Thank you for allowing me to still express that love, for every once in a while, the mother in me gets a glimpse of the little boy I once loved in the strong young man you now love.

"Oh, yes, thank you for allowing me to take pride in you and to love you, too."

Hopefully,

A Good Mother-in-law

STRANGE WAYS TO LEARN ABOUT RELATIONSHIPS

Recently I was talking with a preacher. Now he wasn't my Favorite Preacher Husband or my Favorite Preacher Son. Granted during this particular son's growing up days, there were times when he was not even my favorite son.

Our conversation went something like this, "I write about my grandchildren because they teach me about God."

His response was, "Yes, I know. That is called Toddler Theology."

Since I haven't been to the seminary, I wasn't sure if "Toddler Theology" is correct or not. Just in case it's not, I'm going to use "Traveling Theology" today.

TRAVELING THEOLOGY

What do you do when you travel? We have good friends who listen to book tapes. Others, like my husband, listen to music--all kinds of music from Pete Fountain to Tex Ritter.

One Sunday morning as my husband and I traveled to church I read road signs. They turned into theological thoughts about God and reached out and grabbed me. I was trying to focus on the Sunday School lesson I was to teach from the book of Deuteronomy about how God relates to each of us, but with little success.

GOD RELATES AT MY POINT OF NEED

I have come to know through experience that God relates to me at the point of my need, revealing different facets of Himself in different ways on different days. For instance, this day as we traveled I found myself walking on a tightrope of conflicting feelings and emotions. I've been on this tightrope before and I hate it.

I knew it would claim all my attention and drain me. Closing my eyes (now that may be a dangerous thing to do, especially if you find yourself on a tightrope) I asked God to get me off right now. He didn't.

Instead, through the road signs, He reminded me; He repaired me; He taught me; and He embraced me. The signs were:

Wrong Way

I knew my thinking was stupid. It was good to know He agreed with me. It was no way for a Christian to respond to a frustrating, no-win experience. It was wrong.

Repair Work Ahead

I was given hope to realize God can and would forgive and repair my heart and my influence. All I had to do was to let Him up on the tightrope with me.

Litter Control

My part was to get rid of all the litter: my way, my feelings and my self-centeredness. I think you do this by focusing on others who may need help on their own personal tightrope.

Come Grow With Us

Assurance came in knowing with the help of the Holy Spirit and the sacrifice of His Son, I can continue growing into a fruit-filled and fruit-sharing believer.

Fireworks

I needed to feel the fireworks of the faith hidden away by my silent, tension-filled tightrope walking.

Shady Acres

Finally getting off that tightrope, I found acres of shade in the shadow of the cross and in His agape love. You do know that agape love is love that loves without any thought of return. It just loves.

As we listen, He speaks. He speaks through our Bible, our preachers, our friends, our praise, our grandchildren and our road signs along the way. Don't forget to read the signs today.

I'm not sure if that's good theology or not. But one thing I do know, I'm not hanging on to that emotional tightrope for dear life any more. Traveling Theology worked for me.

The Most Important Relationship
of Your Lifetime

From Faithful Uncle Nelson

I feel cheated. This morning I read from Romans 1: 11-12 (NKJV) these words, "I want to share a spiritual blessing with you. Both you and I will be helped at the same time. You by my faith and I by your faith."

A Writer's Loss

This writing I do every week is really one-sided. I get to share my faith with you, but I'm missing the blessing of your faith. That's definitely my loss.

I did have a unique experience recently of having a 100-year-old gentleman share his faith with me.

He lives in Goss, Mississippi, and his name has always been Uncle Nelson Prescott to me. Now follow this closely -- he's my husband's mother's father's brother! (I was never good at keeping all that straight.)

Eavesdropping on a Conversation

When we arrived in Goss, I saw a vivacious gentleman eating a big piece of pecan pie. Would you like to eavesdrop on the conversation?

"The first time I ever voted was for Woodrow Wilson. I could talk for weeks and never get through, but I better finish eating this pie." He was asked, "What is the secret for keeping your weight down?"

No Secrets Here

"No secret," he said with a smile. "Just quit eating so much and go fishing every chance you get. If I had known I would live to be 100, I might have fished less and written a book." He may not have written a book, but he is a master craftsman in the art of calligraphy, having begun his study in the art in Kansas City in 1910.

"Tell us about your parents, Uncle Nelson."

"Well, my daddy hauled logs during the Civil War. He never got to go to school, but he gave me timber worth $300 to buy half interest in a business college in Hattiesburg, Miss."

Pausing, he said, "Wait a minute. I got off track. (Short pause.) Now I'm back on it. My granddaddy fought in the War of 1812. He was from Georgie, and my grandmother was from Flordie."

There was one time in our conversation that Uncle Nelson never got off track. That was when he told us when he got saved from being lost.

THIS WAS HIS COMPLETE STORY:

"When I was 18, I was a little rowdy, drinking whiskey and fighting in the cotton patch. Ma was always praying that all her children would get saved and join the church.

"One Sunday I walked down and told the preacher I wanted to join the church. I shouldn't have said that. I really thought he was going to refuse me. We talked for a long time about becoming a Christian by believing and trusting in Jesus. Then I was a-crying. I'll never forget it."

His voice broke and he had to wipe the tears away. Continuing, he told us, "When we finished talking, I looked up and Charlie, Bud and Pete had followed me."

"Were you baptized, Uncle Nelson?"

"I was baptized in December, 1906, by old Brother Cox in a creek out from Morgantown."

"No, Uncle Nelson, surely not in the month of December."

Impatiently he repeated, "I was baptized in December, 1906. Pa built a big fire out there by the creek, and as soon as I got out of that cold water, I headed toward it. Up to then, I had given Ma some pain. I straightened up after that."

REMEMBERING RELATIONSHIP THROUGH UNCLE NELSON'S STORY

That night I prayed, "Father, thank You for another rich experience with one of Your special children. Am I giving anyone some pain? If so, help me to straighten this out. Thank you that on May 26, 1948, I was baptized at Second Avenue Baptist Church in Laurel, Miss. to symbolize my new relationship with You through your Son. I pray tonight for those who have no date to remember. Amen."

CHAPTER FIVE:

Solving Pesky Puzzles of Life

I dumped out all the pieces of a large puzzle and took a look. These thoughts entered my mind. "This is a mess; it overpowers me. I just bet you some pieces are missing, too."

Does my puzzle mess remind you of your life today? Maybe you are overpowered by responsibilities and problems. The picture on the lid of the box doesn't make sense either. I hope my columns on puzzle solving will help you put the pieces of your life back together today.

1. Is Your Life One Big Rough Draft?
2. The Lost and Found Column
3. How to Plant a Garden by One Who Never Has
4. Solving the Puzzle of Clutter
5. Time Out is Part of Life's Puzzles

IS YOUR LIFE ONE BIG ROUGH DRAFT?

This I remember. She was a new student. Obviously, I had failed to make the writing assignment clear.

"Mrs. Buckley, just what is a rough draft?"

"What is a rough draft? You have one in your hand; we've been working on it for over a week."

"Oh."

"What you need to do is take your rough draft with all its corrections and improvements and rewrite it before you leave."

At the end of the period the new student hurried up to me and announced with pride, "I've done it. Here's my smooth draft."

She may have been confused about the wording, but her choice of words could help us understand the need for closures in our lives.

THE ROUGH DRAFTS OF OUR LIVES

Do you ever feel your entire life is one big rough draft? Absolutely nothing has any closures. No gate to shut. No "Finished" sign to post. No smooth completed draft to turn in.

I write, knowing in another country, the sounds of bombs are exploding. Our country is at war. Times of adversity are leaving ugly marks on the drafts of so many peoples' lives. War is no respecter of persons. It affects us all: mothers, fathers, lovers and children. I know this first hand. Because of a World War, I grew up never having an opportunity to say the word "Daddy."

How can we become part of the answers to our prayers for peace and protection for those on the front lines and their families? Those front lines may include other areas of living aside from war: business failure, family feuding, health issues or the functioning of our faith.

HOW TO GET UP WHEN YOU FALL DOWN

There is a book called the Bible that reminds me, "If one falls down, his friend can help him up. But pity the man who falls down and has no one to help him up."

May I paraphrase this to read, "If one gets bogged down in his rough draft, friends can help smooth it out. But pity the man who gets bogged down and has no one to smooth the way for him."

LOOK FOR AN ERASER

What are some practical ways we can help smooth the rough times for those who lack closure in their lives? We can listen. Listen to their fears, listen to their questions, listen to their confusion. We can listen even though we have no pat answers. Don't judge. Don't preach. Just listen. You don't have to be an expert to listen.

Then haul off and do something unexpected. Invite them and their anxiety over for a cup of coffee and a hug. Send a card. Write a personal note. Use the phone. Be a source of encouragement.

Next, go and find an eraser. Erase all hard feelings between you and your anxious friends. Keep in mind they may be more argumentative and hard to get along with because of their frustration and helplessness.

On one hand, getting involved in a cause you think is noble might lead to a protest march or a rally to show support. On the other hand, getting involved with the hurts of those around you on a one-to-one basis may cost even more.

HOW TO GET THAT "A"

Dare we think of someone right now who is experiencing a bad time? Let them know you care about their rough draft days. This might enable you to turn in a smooth draft of caring. I think you would receive an A on your paper for sure. Class dismissed.

THE LOST AND FOUND COLUMN

It had been lost for about 10 years. Today I found it. The happening was a sudden discovery. Yet, I knew it existed but wasn't sure where it was or when it got lost.

No, it wasn't The Lost Colony. It was The Lost Column written in Black Mountain, North Carolina in 1994, but it never got published.

Reading over my lost column, I realized it was all about finding something lost, too. May I share this column from the past with you today? I wrote:

DO YOU HAVE A LOST SECRET PLACE?

"What caused my heart to beat faster; my mind to move; my senses to come alive? I found the secret place! Let me start over. In my collection of dreams there had always been a perfect writing spot … a spot where you didn't have to write 'on the run.' (Maybe you don't need a quiet writing spot, but all of us are in need of a quiet place, a blank page or larger margins in our lives.)"

I continued to write:

"I have arrived at my secret place and am ready to enjoy the experience. This perfect environment of a quiet wrap-around porch filled with old rockers, majestic mountains in the distance and no school bells ringing will allow me time to poke around for a while and not be in a hurry.

ARE YOU THE HURRY-UP EXPERT?

"For sure, I am not an expert on this poking around. If you are like me, neither are you. But we are experts in how to do things in a hurry. Most days I find myself:

- Eating in a hurry

- Rushing to get dressed

- Speeding down the road

- Flying into the classroom

- Pushing my students

- Storming into a grocery store

- Throwing something into a microwave

THE ONE THING NOT TO BE HURRIED

"Nevertheless, there is one thing you can never hurry. That is a relationship. Let me repeat. You can never hurry a relationship. It takes time to ripen and get sweet. Long hours are needed for it to grow. Real relationships must include: days meant just for fun, for spinning like a top; days beginning with a dance and ending with a splash of tears; days for hiding your anger, and days for sharing a song; days filled with burning shame and days allowing us to prod someone with praise.

LISTEN TO ONE WHO HAS BEEN THERE, DONE THAT

"Still, there is one relationship which will take an entire lifetime developing. It is never boring or unforgiving or incomplete. This relationship is with the living God Who fully understands us because of His Son's journey to this earth. Because He came, no matter what road we are traveling down today, He knows our pain and loneliness and loss.

"Why? He knew His Father's heart. He knew enough to love. He knew love could not be hurried. He knew real love always pleased the Father, and that was the goal of His unhurried life.

"I never remember Him saying, 'Hurry up and love me.'

"I do remember these words, 'Come, follow me. I will give you rest.'

AN UNHURRIED WALK WITH HIM

"Following Him takes a lifetime. Would you join me today in this discovery of an unhurried walk? Could we make a commitment to stop loving our family and our friends on the run? Even more so, could we stop trying to love our Heavenly Father on the run? If we do, it will be the best discovery we will ever make.

"One final thought … please do not keep this a secret. Share it with all you run into today!"

How to Plant a Garden by One Who Never Has

Once upon a time I was invited to give a "little talk." Understand it wasn't a "motivational speech." It was just a little talk that rambled and strolled around with a nice group of folks.

Props for Planting

We ended up talking about planting a garden, which I had never done. But, I had props--a basket of corn, squash, turnips, lettuce and peas (so I thought). To begin this little talk I held up the lettuce and said something like this:

"Let us be kind to each other. Let us be unselfish. Let us share our memories."

Holding up the squash, I encouraged those gathered to:

"Squash hard feelings. Squash feeling sorry for their selves. Squash rumors."

The turnips were used to remind us we could:

"Turn up for activities. Turn up with a positive attitude. Turn up with a will to do our best."

A Problem Erupts

Finally, I got to the peas. Holding one up, I declared we had to plant three rows of peas ...

That's when the voice interrupted me, "Lady, that's definitely not a pea. My dear, that is a bean."

Laughter erupted. Sure enough, he was right. Nevertheless, we had to plant three rows of peas.

Pleasantness, patience, and perseverance were dropped neatly into three straight rows.

I dislike wasting food, so we need to plant those beans. Do you think we can come up with three thoughts related to beans? Here goes. What about...

"I've 'bean' meaning to loose some weight."

"I've 'bean' meaning to clean out my closet."

"I've 'bean' meaning to get back to church."

LOSING THE WONDER OF PLANTING

I would imagine today that some of you might have lost the WONDER of going to church. Did I ever lose the wonder of going to church? Sure I did. At times, I also lost the wonder of teaching school, of writing, of being a mother and a wife. Did I quit? Did I give up? Did I quit planting?

No. As imperfect as the teaching profession is at times, I didn't quit. I just retired after 32 exciting years. As lousy as it is at times to be a wise mother, mother-in-law, grandmother, I have never quit. As hard as it is on occasion to preserve a strong marriage, I'm still hanging in there after 50 years of being married to my favorite preacher. I'm even still trying to "birth this baby" of being a writer.

PERFECT GARDEN

I am not trying to defend motherhood, or the home, or the school system, or the writing profession, or the church today. Not one of them is perfect. Yet, how empty and incomplete my life would be without their existence. I need my family. I need my church. I need to teach. I must write.

One quick afterthought: I read somewhere that words perish, but deeds re-echo and live through the ages. So much for "little talks" when it's really "little deeds" that count.

SOLVING THE PUZZLE OF CLUTTER

I am surrounded by it. It follows me night and day. No matter how hard I try to escape it, I cannot.

What got me thinking about this was the other day I went to a friend's home and couldn't find it in her house or her yard. Even her kitchen table was free of it. It had nothing on it. Absolutely nothing.

It made me feel really bad. I would love to have a table like that. One free of clutter. Come to think about it, I would love to have a closet, a drawer, a carport, a purse, or a school room without clutter.

DON'T YOU DARE LOOK ON MY KITCHEN TABLE

At this moment, on my kitchen table you could find three coffee cups, two Bibles, a stack of pictures, a bottle of vitamins, a calendar, a thought-for-the-day pad, my Sunday purse, my Sunday School books, four recipes, newspaper clippings, and that's not all.

Let me tell you what happened in my cluttered world last week … something that had never happened before. My favorite preacher bought me one of those new little cars!

My big old car - named the Green Thing by my sixth graders - was born in 1974. She survived many young'uns, many miles and many battle scars. The front seat was ripped, the paint was dull and chipped, and every time it rained I got wet sitting inside the car, not outside it.

MY CLUTTERED GREEN THING AND ME

One school teacher friend said to me, "You know a person's car and their personality usually go together, don't you?" My response was, "I can't believe you said that! Are you comparing me to the cluttered Green Thing?"

Later, I came to the conclusion that the comparison was okay. I am a cluttered person. There, I've admitted it. There's absolutely nothing sterile about me or my surroundings. I am a clutternite.

Rules for Being A True Clutternite

Don't look that word up. I just made it up. Are you a clutternite too? Here are the rules:

- A clutternite has precious possessions – her countless pictures of family and friends, her plants and flowers, her desk, her well-marked Bibles and books, her gentle tiredness at the end of a busy.

- A clutternite is satisfied with her home. Its coziness and familiarity subdue all the flaws and blemishes even as love silences vanity and indifference.

- A clutternite can't quite figure out why folks are always getting in a stew about 'most everything in their lives. These folks seem to be saying, "But we have to worry!" She answers, "Why?" Trust, not worry, is her password.

Clutternites Take Time for Relationships With Others

- A clutternite takes time to dream and swing. She hugs you and listens to you. She actually looks at you and sees your hurts and dullness, smells the spices and fragrance of your life.

- A clutternite has time for her children, her mother and her dog. She values her husband's happiness. She values her friends and herself.

- A clutternite is pure comfort and all embracing. Just as she embraces her cluttered possessions, she embraces you with acceptance and love on her unhurried pace through life with her family and her God.

- A clutternite has no off limits or closed rooms in her life. Her home is an open as her heart. There's no fear that you might mess things up in her world because it is already scattered with the proof of real living.

- A clutternite takes the time to know God, talk with God and enjoy God. She sees Him in the hills as they break forth into singing, and she hears Him in the trees of the fields as they clap their hands in praise! (Isaiah 55:12)

If you ever meet a true clutternite, please let me know. I would like to stroll happily along with them and enjoy their spontaneity, their humor and their clutter.

Time Out is Part of Life's Puzzles

Without a shadow of a doubt, we have one need in common. That one need could be a dire craving for money. No, that is not the answer. What about power and control? No, that's not it either. It must be religion. The answer is still no.

No? Isn't this a religion column? Wait and see.

Now waiting is not normally on our Things-To-Do-List, is it? Many of us just move that mouse to "Cancel" when "Wait" comes up on the screens of our life.

A Friendly Beep-Beep Reminder

Hopefully these words are a friendly "beep-beep" reminding you to take time to simply pause for short periods of time in your busy days. Just for today stop being a flawless, tidy, efficient robot. Maybe you think your world will collapse if you don't hold it up. That is not so; and with that thought we identify our shared need. It is to call "time out" and regroup, relax, and be revitalized.

Stop Trying To Impress Others

Can't do it? Why not? Maybe you think you must always be performing to impress others. There is nothing more exhausting than constantly putting yourself on that stage. Instead, may I suggest you take time to hover and hum and listen to the slow drumming beat of life? This beat can be heard in all your relationships with God, others and yourself in service to Him.

Just For Today

Just for today take time to:
Skip as you steal a happy moment or as you are stabbed with pain.
Smile as you slump over and come to a complete stop.
Just for today take time to:
Weep as you walk or wait quietly.
Laugh as you lag behind or leap forward.

Just for today take time to:

Ponder as to why you are being punched or pampered.

All are necessary. All mesh together as part of living. All will visit us. The question is, "What will be our reaction to their visit?"

Yet, the most far-reaching visit ever made to me, as a Christian, was when God, in Christ Jesus, visited our earth and invited me home with Him to be with the Father today and forever.

I accepted the invitation many years ago, and my greatest everlasting need was met. Have you? Why don't you take time to ponder that grand invitation right now and share it with someone?

Putting Some Good on Our 50th Wedding Anniversary Celebration on August 2, 2009 with our Friends and Family

BILLIE AND GERALD

OUR SONS, STEVE AND STAN

THE WHOLE GANG

STEVE AND KRISTI

STEVE AND FAMILY

STAN AND JEWELL

STAN AND FAMILY

ADAM, NEAL AND SLADE, ANNA, ANNALEIGH

ANNA AND ANNALEIGH

CHAPTER SIX:

Growing Up Days

I have a long-standing love affair. No, it is not illegal or immoral. It is a love affair with my childhood. The values of my growing-up years were quite different from the values shared by kids of today.

Today "pretending" is a lost art. For me, playing was for fun ... not for competing to be an all-star or a whatever. You sang for the pure joy of it ... not for a trophy.

Have we robbed our children of a childhood free from evaluations and rewards? Have we gone too far in the praising that says, "I love you because ...?"

My challenge is to change all that praise-pandering to simple words of encouragement. Try this: "You worked hard and did a good job." That will do it.

Join me in these next columns to be reminded of your past and how to make a difference in the present for the future.

1. Running the Race of Love
2. Pretending is a Thing of the Past
3. Wishing From a Sears Roebuck Catalogue
4. My Mother's True Grit
5. Reflections on My Granny Howard
6. Reflections on Biscuits and Daffodils and Grandma Beulah

Do you remember those childhood races of long ago? I do. They are part of my love affair with my childhood.

Drive down to Laurel, Mississippi with me. Let's find First Avenue. Now we have to look for 1924 First Ave. That's where my races took place.

On a hot summer day you would find me (Billie Jean), Paul Jr., Ouida, Bo and Mamie Rea all barefooted and lined up for the race.

One of us would be "It" and call out: "ON YOUR MARK! GET SET! GO!"

We took off, never feeling the thorns and stickers hidden in our front yard race track. We took off with energy and the love of the race. Strange, but I don't remember who was the fastest runner. It wasn't important to us. We simply ran for the love of it.

Today, with that same energy and love, I want us to race from "You got to be kidding, Lord!" to "Now I got it, Father!" I finally understand this idea, this feeling and this action of love from my Father's point of view. My first lesson was:

"CONSIDER THE LILIES HOW THEY GROW." LUKE 12: 27 (KJV)

My response: "Father, You have to be kidding! I know when Jesus used the word 'lilies' He was referring to the wild flowers scattered along the wayside. I also know most folks don't see them at all; and surely this part of Your creation never fusses over their outward appearances. My world today fusses over being seen, being well-dressed, being well-off. These fussy people are filled with such harshness and 'tricks of the trade.' They even apply it to Your work. So when I consider the lilies, do you mean for me to not fuss over outward appearances and depend on You to grow me?"

His reply: "My child, you are almost there. I have a lot of lilies out there getting overlooked by the world. You need to find them for Me and love and encourage them just for Me. Don't forget, in all your business for Me, to look for My lilies."

My response: "Finally, now I got it! I'm to be like the lilies in that they depend on their Creator to grow them. As my Creator, grow me to be more like Your Son who never overlooked the lilies in need of love. Do you have anything else to teach Me about Your love?

"YOU TELL PEOPLE ABOUT ME EVERYWHERE." ACTS 1:8 (NKJV)

My response: "You have to be kidding! Is that what You really want me to do...to tell Your story? That scares me. What if I mess it up? What if they don't want to hear Your story? What if they stop liking me for bringing it up? Okay, just what do You want me to tell them?"

His reply: "Even though you are a writer, tell them you are not the author of the story of my love. You are just my errand person to remind them I love them; tell them I want them to come home. Don't forget to tell them I have prepared a way for their homecoming. Then I want you to be living proof of what Jesus can do for them and in them. Out of the fullness of your heart you speak and write of Me and My love"

My response: "Father, finally I got it! You want me to bear fruit. As I understand this, I bring You and others together through my prayers and my actions of love. Then Your Holy Spirit can have more room to work in their lives. It also moves Satan back off the playing fields of their lives so You can have more room to work Your love, too. Right? Is the track to put Your story on inside me? Is it an overflow of Your love, joy, peace, patience, goodness, gentleness, mercy, faithfulness and self-in-step-with-You? How can I keep silent when others are crying out, 'Tell me the old, old story of Jesus and His love?'"

I think I understand the race of love better now: it's being one with You in my mind, motives and movement. Are You telling us today to get our minds "ON YOUR MARK" for the quest to find your lilies, and to "GO" as your errand person to love them for You? That is one race I want to run in spite of all the "thorns and stickers" of hate out there.

PRETENDING IS A THING OF THE PAST

It's lost. It doesn't exist today. What have we lost? Pretending is a lost art because our children don't know how to pretend any more.

GROWING UP IN THE PAST

Growing up, I cut paper dolls out of catalogues. I made mud pies and frosted them with wild flowers or pebbles. I created playhouses out of boards and sticks. I can't remember seeing a child do this recently. Maybe it's because there is no need to pretend anymore. Children today have the real things--real dolls, real ovens and real play houses.

On the other hand, some things about our childhood have not changed. The innocent conversations of children are still reasons for us to stop, smile and think. In the book, *A Monster is Bigger than 9,* we can eavesdrop on some thought-provoking exchanges by children. Listen carefully to this conversation:

"LET'S PRETEND YOU LIKE ME, OKAY? IF YOU DO WE CAN TAP DANCE IN THE SANDBOX."

Would you agree there are some folks you know who just don't want to play with in the sandbox? For one thing, they don't know how to play. Never would you see them get on the floor with a child, much less in a sandbox.

TURN IT AROUND

If we turn this around, we might be identified as the one whom others have to pretend they like. We may never get invited to put on our dancing shoes because we are too bossy and demanding, or we are too negative and angry.

If we refrain from throwing stinging darts, I don't think we will have to say, "Let's pretend you like me, okay?" People will genuinely like you.

Moving On

Let's move on. I see two little girls with their heads close together, sharing a secret. One jumps up, puts her hands on her hips and shares a hurt, "She screamed me over today."

Have you ever been screamed over by the blow of sharp words?

This is a blow that is hard to recover from. When words are screamed at us it may cause us to lose our confidence in the person God created us to be.

If we refrain from throwing stinging darts, I don't think we will have to say, "Let's pretend you like me, okay?" People will genuinely like you. The last pretending thought goes like this:

"Let's pretend we're having fun."

Do you have to *pretend* to have fun? Is there anything in your life you *truly* enjoy doing? Why not let the child in you come on out and play? I guarantee you the "pretending" will slink away and the child in you will skip back into your life and dance in the sandbox.

WISHING FROM A SEARS ROEBUCK CATALOGUE

Growing up I made wishes from the Sears Roebuck catalogue. Nowadays I made wishes from a computer. Recently I have ordered presents on my computer, and I've begun to have dreams about putting good on others' lives through my very own web site.

HOW I KNEW CHRISTMAS WAS COMING

As a child there was no computer, no television, no car, no air-conditioning … only my Mother and me. But every year I knew Christmas was coming. I could feel it. I could see it. I could hear it. Children have this magic sense for the season. This excitement mounted in me as a child when I saw those blue glass Christmas balls decorating the slender silver tree in our small squared-off living room.

Remember, the Sears Roebuck catalogue was my wish book. At times I cut out lovely ladies and handsome gentlemen from catalogues for my paper dolls. But never did I cut out a picture in the Christmas issue. It was special. It gave my dreams a chance to come true.

MY ONE CHRISTMAS WISH

This particular Christmas I had only one wish. That wish was for a bride doll; a doll dressed in a lacy, white, long flowing gown. It was rich and beautiful, representing everything we did not have. Oh, we were rich in love but not rich in material possessions. Remember, it was just my Mother and me. My Father had died in Germany during World War II.

THE SLOW PACE OF CHRISTMAS COMING

Christmas was slow getting there. At last Christmas Eve arrived. Going to sleep on that night for a child is almost an impossible task. Your eyes won't close, your mind won't shut down and your covers won't stay on. Your ears are wide awake, listening for the magic sounds of the season.

I wonder if the Sears Roebuck catalogue is being published any more. If it isn't, maybe we can just wish from our hearts.

My Christmas Wishes for You This Year

I wish for you:

- to double the pleasure of your life even as our five grandchildren have done for us

- a freshness in all you do and a return of the goose bumps and shivers

- the ability to let go of all the hurts, making room for the joys of the coming season

- a whole calendar full of God's presence

The Greatest Gift Giver

Now my best wish for you this Christmas is you might desire to know the God of Christmas in a more personal way. This one thing I know about Him. He is the greatest gift-giver this world has ever known. As a Christian, I believe His great gift to all mankind was Himself in the character of His Son, whose birthday we celebrate on Christmas Day.

God had His love to be born of woman. In the manger His love became my hope. On the cross His love became my substitute for that which separates me from God. The Bible calls this sin. The world calls it foolishness. I call His name Jesus.

Show and Tell Many Years Later

A few years ago, we had "Show and Tell Time" in my sixth grade class as a pre-writing activity. Guess what I brought to school for Show and Tell? A bride doll whose dress was yellow with age and torn from much loving! Tonight she sits proudly on my bed, reminding me of the magic of a long-ago Christmas, the other joys of Christmas past and the hope of Christmases to come. I know you have a Christmas story in you, too. Share it with your children and grandchildren today. That is my final wish for you.

My Mother's True Grit

Dear Grandchildren,

I write today to share with you part of your roots. I called her Mother for 76 years. Your dads called her Ma. She loved your fathers and would have loved you, too. This is the first lesson you may learn from her. Never once did she boo her family or forget to applaud loudly for us. I hope you learn this well.

She Played by the Rules

Her home was one of order. In fact, order was part of her make-up. She probably never went over the speed limit or ran a stop sign her entire life. You may learn the design of an ordered life from her.

All her life was kept in bounds. She played by the rules. She was a polite, precise, church- loving lady. She never cheated or cut corners. You may learn the value of honesty from her.

She took delight in a job well done. Her standards were high. One example of her quality workmanship is the beautiful quilts in all our homes. You may learn the pursuit of excellence from her.

Loyalty Part of Her Character

Loyalty was part of her character. She was loyal to my father's parents after his death, her church, her family and to me. She never thought of herself as a big deal. Always, you could find her in the background of any picture. I will look for that loyalty in your lives as you grow up.

The greatest lesson you may learn from her is how to survive with "true grit." It took real grit to send a young husband off to war in the 1940's. Grit and grace were needed to raise a daughter all by yourself after receiving the "I regret to inform you ..." letter from our government.

She Made a Great Comeback

Never was this "true grit" more evident than in the comeback from her first stroke. The second stroke, six months later, left her with no power to fight before she died. I have to tell you a secret. She was a "scaredy cat" when it came to doing some things alone. So when I knew God was going to take her home to live with Him, I asked Him to send 10,000 angels to come and get her. At times, I still hear those angel wings in my heart.

Let's Follow Her Example

I'm grateful on this Mother's Day she passed through my life as my Mother. I hope she will pass through me into your life and the cycle will not be broken in you, my grandchildren … Adam, Neal, Anna, Slade and Annaliegh. Listen closely and you just might hear those angel wings even now.

Write Your Own Loving Legacy

P.S. Have you written a "this I remember letter" to your grandchildren lately? I hope my letter will encourage you to do so. A loving legacy left in a letter needs to be read, celebrated and lived out from one generation to another.

REFLECTIONS ON MY GRANNY HOWARD

*S*he was no saint. Never would she want me to leave that impression. She was a survivor, having survived the death of her parents, her husband, all 13 brothers and sisters and three children. She survived depressions, wars and every president from William McKinley to William Jefferson Clinton.

In one of the many cards she sent to me, Granny wrote about her home. "God is so good to me and I try to give Him all the praise for everything. I have never been able to buy a home of my own, and God never saw fit to give me one on this earth. But He has one for me in heaven much more beautiful than any fine home on this earth. That gives me peace and great joy past understanding."

When she was 86 years old she was sent an appreciation card. Inside were these words, "For teaching the Teen Class in Bible School, July 22-26, 1985." She knew that Bible well, having read through it 36 times. As we celebrated her 90th birthday in 1990 she remained opinionated and alert in mind and spirit.

In 1996 she wrote instructions concerning arrangements for her funeral. She closed with these words. "I cannot leave anything but the same thing my father and mother left me. I have treasured it above all the gold or riches in this world. It is a belief in a living God and an assurance to be home with Him soon. This is all I can offer to anyone. This belief has been a good friend to me."

Postscript: My Granny, Mrs. Verna Howard went home March 17, 1997. We celebrated her life and homecoming. She was 97 years young. She is buried in Laurel, Mississippi.

REFLECTIONS ON BISCUITS AND
DAFFODILS AND GRANDMA BEULAH

Could we celebrate today? What are we celebrating? How about celebrating the coming of spring and today I saw a yellow daffodil.

I tell this story simply because I must. It is my tribute to the simple, good people who lived and died unnoticed and not applauded by the world.

I never see a daffodil that I don't think about my Grandma Beulah. She was my father's mother. She had no running water and only a wood stove; but on Sunday mornings we would get up to hot biscuits. There was a special way to eat those biscuits at her house. You poured your syrup over a gob of white butter fresh from the churn. Then you took your fork and beat the syrup and butter together. Finally, you took that hot biscuit and sopped up the syrup and butter. Sometimes you poked a whole in the top of the biscuit and poured the syrup and butter in the hole. Never could you eat just one. Before you left for church, she would always tell me, "Billie Jean, go get your Sunday shoes so we can shine them." Then she would take a leftover biscuit and rub it over my black patent leather shoes.

I never understood why she did that because we always had to walk down a dusty road past her field of daffodils, the old barn and a storm pit to get to Ted Baptist Church in Louin, Miss. I forgot to tell you, she always sent a fruit jar of those daffodils with me on my way to Sunday School.

Fast forward this story. I am now all grown up with a family of my own. I still go to church. One day I had kept the nursery at our church in Natchez, Miss. That particular Sunday afternoon the phone rang. Our friend Cathy called to say Amanda, her three year old, had been fussing since she got home from church.

Her voice was filled with frustration. She said to me, "Billie, Amanda keeps telling me she wants me to cook her a biscuit so she can polish her shoes, and you told her she could!"

Laughing, I tried to explain, "Well, Cathy, Amanda is right. It's like this … many years ago; I had a Grandma Beulah …"

CHAPTER SEVEN:

In the Classroom
for 32 Years

Many years ago in Pontotoc, Mississippi, I got a short note from my principal. She wrote, "I like your room. The witches are not all flying the same way." To this day it frightens me to walk in a classroom, a home, a church or a community where all the youth are encouraged to color the same picture, the same way, with the same color. It was hard to choose only five columns out of my many teaching columns, but these I have chosen for your pleasure.

1. Thoughts From the Last Days of School
2. Be Careful What You Ask Your Students
3. What All Students Have in Common
4. Let Your Kids Use Every Color in the Box
5. Three Things Students Wonder About

Thoughts From the Last Days of School

Many years ago in Pontotoc, Mississippi, I got a short note from my principal. She wrote, "I like your room. The witches are not all flying the same way."

What Frightens You as a Teacher?

To this day it frightens me to walk in a classroom, a home, a church, or a community where all the youth are encouraged to color the same picture, the same way, with the same color.

The Walls of Education Will Not Fall Down

As a teacher for 32 years, starting in North Carolina and ending at Petal, Mississippi, I gave my students permission to color outside the lines as long as it was not harmful to themselves or to others. It was okay in my room for them to politely question me, to express doubts and to not be ashamed of their differences.

Never did I fear the "walls of education" would fall down if every single student did not understand and work every single math problem on the board at the same time.

When Does Real Learning Take Place?

I am afraid we as parents, teachers, and coaches are organizing away our youths' days to the point of denying them growing-up time. I frankly can't organize a two-car parade. But I can tell you when real learning took place in my room. Understand this was before the days of teaching controlled by the necessity of testing.

It was when I said, "Here it is. Have at it. Today there will be no pretests, no post-tests, no computer tests, no analysis, no graphs on your progress, no grades, no seat work and no home work." I was well aware if this wasn't done at an appropriate time and in an appropriate way, there would be no job for Mrs. Buckley.

Same Idea Invades my Faith

The same principles applied to my teaching also invade the sharing of my faith. It is strong enough to allow for communication and exchange of ideas.

Those who would give a rebuttal to my words are far more sophisticated and "spiritual" than I. They are masters of rhetoric and persuasion. I could not even persuade Fritz, our overweight dachshund, to go outside when it rained. I've certainly never preached to thousands…only two sons for 44 years. Nor have I ever held a press conference, unless you could count a second grader interviewing me one day many years ago.

It is evident my credentials on this stand are not impressive. But the one fact I do know is the God of this universe is not threatened by our struggles, our doubts, our differences or our uniqueness.

Learning to Build Bridges

In His wisdom God built a bridge from each individual heart to His heart. May we as parents, educators and friends of the youth of our land learn to build bridges. We must not stop there. This bridge building must be taught and carried on from one generation to another. So be it!

P.S. Teachers, use the summers to stop and rest from the demands of the classroom; but never use it to stop teaching.

Be Careful What You Ask Your Students

Teachers, the end is near. I remember the end of my 30th year of teaching. My mother had died, one fellow teacher had cancer and another died suddenly at school. My students had to grow up fast that year. Yet, as always I asked for an evaluation from my 135 or so students. This is a dangerous thing to do. Children are honest. But teachers must be brave. Open your heart and enjoy!

What Did You Like About This Room?

"I liked the paper shoot-out the best. The only bad part was when I finally got good, school ended."

"What I mean is… there was respect in this room. I liked that."

"The Thought for the Day was the best. It helped me change my attitudes."

"I like this class because you weren't concerned about school stuff all the time. When something was going on in the world we could talk about it in here"

What Are Ways This Class Could Be Improved?

"I think you should let us write more poems even if you aren't a poet."

"I think you should take that yellow thing off your desk."

"You should let us sit down in any desk we want to."

"It should stay the same except for the closet that things fall out of when you open the door."

What Have You Learned About Grammar and Writing?

"I learned they are not so boring after all."

"I learned about double negatives, subject verb agreement and good hooks."

"I learned to have a visual point of view concerning what you are writing." (Did I teach that? Sounds good to me.)

"This year I learned to speak plain English at all times."

WHAT HAVE YOU LEARNED ABOUT LIFE THIS YEAR?

"One thing is don't tip somebody's bucket over if it has been dripped in all day. They may get mad."

"It's okay to cry when you are sad."

"In order to get ahead you must have… (Mrs. Buckley, what's that word?) That's it. How do you spell it … Integrity?"

"In life I learned I have a lot to learn about life."

As a Christian teacher I hope I learned those same lessons from all those sensational sixth graders I taught. Please don't tell anyone, but at times I miss their humor, their honesty and their enthusiasm.

WHAT ALL STUDENTS HAVE IN COMMON

This I remember. I remember the first days of school when those sixth graders entered my classroom. They all had one thing in common. They were always looking for something. For a few, it was trouble. For others it was a friend, teacher approval, good grades, or a way to escape or outdistance whatever was chasing them. As I look back, through the heart of a teacher, I realized this search most always centered on their need for somebody to understand them.

One spring day we called the writing assignment, "The Real Me." It took place March 22, 1990 in the Petal Middle School. I know the date because the sixth grade writer entered it at the top of her paper. Would you like to understand our children of today in a more defined way? Listen with your heart as you read their writing assignments. You may be surprised what you learn.

THE REAL ME SHOWS OTHERS

"The real me can't be seen from the outside. People I love can only see it. Now I'm not the best there is with all this lovey-dovey stuff. I don't really tell them that stuff, but I try to show them with my actions."

THE REAL ME NO ONE EVER LAUGHS WITH

"No one sees the real me. I am very funny…but no one ever laughs. Not many people even want to see it so I just try to be serious. Sometimes I feel like an encyclopedia. I know a lot but hardly anyone wants to know what I know."

THE REAL ME HIDES SOMETHING

"People see me as a bully or a smart mouth. But the real me is just adventurous. I love to romp the woods and sit down to watch the animals play. I love to make things. I whittle statues out of pinewood or make whistles out of bamboo." (Written the next day:) "I didn't get completed on what I said yesterday. The other side I never let anyone see is an angry side. I hope no one ever sees this side."

THE REAL YOU AS A TEACHER

Do you remember I wrote you might be surprised when you read what my students wrote back in 1990? Teachers, maybe the big surprise was you saw "The Real You" for the first time in my students' writing assignment.

HOW DOES A REAL TEACHER TEACH?

By the way if you are a real teacher … then TEACH. Always remember, the real teacher makes learning a JOY. Now that is not easy unless you have your Masters' joy inside you. Remember happiness is fickle and joy is not.

LET YOUR KIDS USE EVERY COLOR IN THE BOX

The website spotlighted the words in bold letters: **Need Ideas for Back-to-School**? The answer was, "We've put together a list of ideas for kid-pleasing lunches."

LIFE PRIORITIES

May I confess to you this was never a priority in my life, to make kid-pleasing lunches? Now, our sons didn't like this about me on some mornings; but that never was my top priority as a mother either –to get my sons to like me. Shoot, I didn't like them at times either.

I figured it this way: if I ate cafeteria food (for 32 years) it was good enough for them, too. And if I remember correctly, once I bought them little tin lunch boxes and gave them permission to fix their own lunches.

Yet, kids do have certain needs for back-to-school. My, how needs have changed. I read recently where one school required their students to have their own personal laptops. Now I used to get in a "stew" because my students didn't have a pencil.

PERMISSION GRANTED

One back-to-school need our kids have is to be given permission to use all the colors in the box to draw their teacher. Some teachers, including myself, fit the description made by an innocent child. When asked to draw a picture of her teacher, she said quite honestly, "Oh, I can't make a picture of my teacher. I don't have a **gray** color."

What about you, teachers? Will your students only need a gray color to draw you and your teaching: drab, boring, sarcastic? Or could a child use the color **red** because you are alive with energy and enthusiasm? Some days you will have to fake these feelings, but that's alright because enthusiasm for learning is caught from a teacher colored red**.**

What about **blue**? Think about a blue unending sky for this one. At times your patience will have to be unending. Be sure you students see this color in you. When frustrated I always tried to send an I-message and not a you-message. How does that work? Instead of telling the messy student, "You have to clean up around your desk. You are a pig." Put it this way, "I can't function with the mess around your desk. I'm getting old and I work best when there is some order around." It works. It really does (most of the time).

Then there is my granddaughters' favorite color-**pink**. That color reminds me of warmth and concern. I've already reminded our granddaughter there might be a scared little boy or girl in her kindergarten room. She has decided she will be their friend. I hope she has a teacher who is colored pink to set an example of caring for her.

As my sons grew older, they paid me back for not fixing their kid-pleasing lunch by telling everyone, "We love cafeteria food. It's so much better than Mother's cooking"

P.S. I also know cafeteria food really is good now as compared to way back then. In reality, it probably is better than their mother's cooking!

THREE THINGS STUDENTS WONDER ABOUT

One of my recent columns included a paradox; I took my family to a cemetery to celebrate a birthday. Today's story centers on a paradox, too. I begin this story by reminding you I was a school teacher for 32 years. A few weeks ago the roles were reversed. I became the learner.

The schoolroom was a slightly scattered den. The teacher was a three-year-old burning up with fever. Her warm head laid on a pillow and her quiet feet rested in my lap. All was still except her active mind. As we talked, she started counting all the way to the magic number … 100!

I asked her, "Did you learn to count in your pre-school?"

"No, Mam."

"I know. You learned from television."

"No, Mam."

"Then how did you learn to do all that counting?"

"My brother 'teached' me."

How these words connected the dots for me. How she filled in the blanks, causing me to remember. I remembered some of the truths my students "teached" me when I was suppose to be the teacher.

On one particular day the dusty green chalkboard in my sixth grade room instructed my 134 students to write, "Three things I wonder about are…."

DID YOU EVER WONDER WHAT KIDS WONDER ABOUT? WELL, SOME WONDERED:

"How did God become God?"

"Will I ever see my mom?"

"Why doesn't my dad ever write or call?"

"How many fruit combinations are in a bag of Skittles?"

THE CREATIVE ONES WONDERED:

"What is under my bed?"

"What was my mother like as a teenager?"

"Will I ever be able to slam-dunk a basketball?"

THE WORRIED ONES WONDERED:

"Why is junk so expensive?"

"When will I ever get to skate until 12 o'clock?"

"Why don't some people go to church? "

WHAT IS ON YOUR PERSONAL WONDER LIST TODAY?

I have a few, too. They are not original or creative.

I wonder about my grandchildren and their future in relationship to terrorist activities in our world.

I wonder about the movement to remove God's name from our entire heritage.

I wonder how we will teach our children the value of honesty and Godly values based on God's plumb line when the world is trying to erase that plumb line.

YET, THERE IS ONE THING I DO NOT WONDER ABOUT

You see, "I know in whom I have believed. I am persuaded that He is able to keep that which I have committed unto Him against that Day!"

That, my friend, is the Wonder of all Wonders!

CHAPTER EIGHT:
My Yo-Yo Emotions

Please don't think you will ever have it all together. Life will move too fast and change the rules every time you step up to the plate. The only thing that is stable and unending for me is my personal oneness with God who is Holy and my Father; His Son who is my Savior and my Friend; His Holy Spirit who dwells in me and walks before me. That is based on my favorite verse found in Ecclesiastes 4:12 (NKJV) to remind me each day, "A three fold cord is not easily broken." So when I am one with His mind, His motive of love and His movement I will find stability to replace the unsteadiness of life. Many of my columns were honest to the point of being painful in regard to emotions coming and going.

1. Not on My Watch
2. Gratitude Flying with Superman
3. Saying "I 'm Sorry" is Hard
4. Let's Just Skip the Whole Thing!

NOT ON MY WATCH

This column was written August 22, 2007 at Gulf Shores, Alabama, on notebook paper with a #2 pencil. One morning I watched the waves repeatedly tumbling onto the shore … over and over again.

Four words tumbled into my mind as steady as the waves raced to the shore. "Not on my watch. Not on my watch. Not on my watch."

FOUR WORDS POUNDING IN MY MIND

The words were foreign to my style of writing for this newspaper for twenty years. They were too lofty, too zealous and too controversial. Nevertheless, as fast as a new wave formed, the words pounded in my mind and raced onto the notebook paper.

Surely, some sixty years ago, my 24-year-old father who was killed in Germany died with those words in his heart, "Not on my watch will my wife and little girl know evil such as the likes of Hitler."

SPEAKING WITH ONE VOICE

Today could we come together and speak those four words with one voice? What will the world hear us saying?

Parents and grandparents lovingly saying, "Not on my watch will you be applauded or overlooked for your obnoxious, sullen, destructive behavior."

Workers who wearily whisper, "Not on my watch will things be done half-way, half-hearted and half-cocked."

DID I HEAR YOUR VOICE?

Government officials who proudly stand and say, "Not on my watch will corruption and greed take place."

Citizens saying with strength and integrity, "Not on my watch will laziness, playing the system and welfare abuse be rewarded with free hand-out programs." (Please note I said, welfare *abuse* and not just welfare.)

Young people saying together with one voice, "Not on my watch will easy sex, hard liquor, damaging drugs, cheating or lying invade and take over my body, my mind, my actions."

Teachers creating a learning environment by simply stating, "Not on my watch will your individual behavior prevent me from teaching the truths that will eventually set you free from ignorance and the world's warped view of values."

WHAT DID JESUS HAVE TO SAY?

I remember Jesus once asked His disciples, "Could you not watch with me?"

I hope I will recall those pounding waves no longer visible to my eyes. My hope is that their memory will move to my heart and with every beat I will hear, "Not on my watch will evil prevail because I do nothing. I will stand with my Lord on our watch."

I also remember He told one of His frustrated disciples, "Don't you know I must be about my Father's business?"

Today I ask, "Lord, may I walk with You on Your watch as You seek to find Your children and with love bring them home?"

GRATITUDE FLYING WITH SUPERMAN

Thanksgiving is a time to be grateful, and this gratitude has many of the same qualities as Superman. Let's see if we can figure this out together.

GRATITUDE IS ALWAYS ON DUTY AND SO IS SUPERMAN.

Gratitude is on time and in step with the need and so is Superman. Both are "faster than a speeding bullet." Many of us need to speed up expressing our appreciation to others. They may have waited for 30 Novembers to hear you say, "Thank you. You have touched me and I have grown." Is this a lost art? Is it too old fashioned to teach our children and grandchildren? We may also need to give God credit today for the pleasure of His presence in our lives. When this happens we are definitely on course with God's heart.

GRATITUDE IS STRONG AND SO IS SUPERMAN.

Gratitude has strength to go first without other's approval and so does Superman. They are both "stronger than a locomotive." A grateful heart is strong enough and brave enough to take the lead, instead of standing still and waiting for others to move. This waiting around is often done under the guise of being timid; I personally have a hard time with this excuse when it is used for indifference, rudeness, or laziness.

Those who follow the example of our Lord are strong enough to say, "It doesn't matter your response to me. I'll love you … not if you love me, not when you love me, or not because you love me. I'll just love you anyway and show that love through a grateful heart."

GRATITUDE CAN APPLAUD OTHERS AND SO CAN SUPERMAN.

Gratitude possesses certain steady qualities for a strong foundation and so does Superman. They both can "leap over tall buildings in a single bound." Those possessing this steadiness feel comfortable with themselves. This allows them to say to others, "You take a bow and let me applaud you."

The tallest building standing in the way is the opposite of gratitude--arrogance. Arrogant folks think too highly of themselves and need the spotlight focused on their performance instead of those in need of encouragement. I think we play our lives to the wrong audience at times. There is only One whose applause we should desire, and that is our Heavenly Father.

GRATITUDE CAN MOVE FAST WITH ENCOURAGEMENT AND SO CAN SUPERMAN.

Gratitude "talks" with a smile, a thank you, an action of encouragement and so does Superman. Both can walk on water, crawl on land, or fly over oceans to show their thankful heart with appropriate action. Those who follow this sense of direction are doers. They act. They show politeness. They can do this because they have learned one lesson well. They know it is God who is deserving and who is worthy of our best possession. What is that? It is our time. It takes time to talk with God. It takes time to express a courteous thank you. May we never be too busy to pour out our great gratitude to Him for His even greater love for His children!

Oh, yes, I almost forgot. Thank you for encouraging me as a writer for 'nigh' over 20 years. I began writing these columns in 1987.

Saying, "I'm Sorry" is Hard

(A REAL LETTER WRITTEN TO A REAL PUBLIC NONBELIEVER.)

Dear Sir:

As part of organized religion, which is to you a sham and a crutch, I write this letter. Others have asked you to apologize; instead, I would like to say, "I am sorry."

I am sorry that no one has ever told you truthfully about the reality of the Christian religion based on a relationship with its central figure, Jesus Christ.

I am sorry that no one has ever lived before you a life of faith in Him to show you the true God of my faith.

You and I do have one thing in common. No, I have never had my face of the front of Newsweek magazine as a politician. No, I have never been interviewed by Playboy magazine as a flamboyant personality. (I can't spell, it much less be it.)

Yet, in 1979 I wrote a prayer in front of my Bible. I prayed, "Lord, make me real and not religious."

I really don't know you, but you seem to put a lot of stock in being real. May I share with you the reality of the Christian religion, as I understand it?

Am I right to think you share with many others the following objections to Christianity? The first objection is, "The church if filled with hypocrites. It is a sham."

Well, I have to agree with you. There are hypocrites in the church I have loved for over 60 years. On the other hand, there are people of integrity in my church. People who value what God values and not what the world says is valuable.

But, that is not the real issue. I am not asked to follow Christ's followers but to follow Him. Was He a hypocrite? If He was, then my faith is a sham.

All scripture tells me that He was perfect and without sin.

By the way, being a sinner does not make me a hypocrite for this is the first step in becoming a Christian. Simply put, I must recognize that my sins do separate me from God. You might want to know this: Jesus denounced hypocrites even as you do.

Your second objection to organized religion was that it is just a crutch for weak people. **Karl Marx agreed with you. He said, "Religion is the opiate of the masses."**

Strange as it may seem, most folks do need a crutch at some point in their life. Could it be, just maybe, your "in-your-face" personality is a crutch? Surely, the "real you" needs a quiet time away from the noise and the confusion of the sensationalism in the political arena. Just maybe you need a time when you don't have to know the answer to every question … no matter how shallow or how deep.

I think I know why you are confused about this. You may think Christianity is designed for weak people who need an emotional crutch or a blanket of protection. Your strong personality does not recognize this need.

May I share with you my faith in Christ has made me strong as I depend on Him? Now this is not a passive, fold-your-hands, sit-in-the-corner dependence. I would never have survived 32 years in a classroom as a teacher if this were so.

MY CHRISTIAN FAITH CENTERS AROUND THESE WORDS OF JESUS:

"I am the Way (if you get lost, Billie). I am the Truth (even if you are sincerely wrong, it doesn't count, Billie). I am the Light (if you find yourself in the darkness, Billie) No man cometh unto the Father except by me." Now He was either who He said He was, or a lunatic or a liar.

As a nine year old little girl in Laurel, Mississippi, I heard these words and somehow knew I needed a heavenly Father. My earthly father was killed in a foxhole in Germany during World War II. I have learned from his letters and life (as told to me by others) that his faith was not a sham or a crutch.

What a waste his life would have been if this were true. My hope is that your life will not be wasted either.

Respectfully,
Billie Buckley
P.O. Box 113
Petal, MS 39465

Did I hear you Say ... Let's Just Skip the Whole Thing!

Do you have a favorite movie? I do. It's about a friendship between a dog named Otis and a cat named Milo. To really like this movie you must have a child's heart to go along with your grown-up mind.

Open Your Heart and Let the Child in You Out

I know you may be wondering how a story centered on a cat and a dog could have anything to do with personal peace. Let me remind you Jesus used objects to teach great lessons. Now, if we can open your heart and mind and let the kid escape, we may enjoy the journey.

In our movie, it was a beautiful morning. As Otis marched down the road he was heard chanting, "Here comes the dog brave and strong and....!" With the last word trailing off, the confident Otis fell into a deep hidden hole in the middle of the road. Crawling out, a bit tattered and torn, he muttered. "Let's just skip the whole thing."

There are Holes Out There Waiting for You.

I can't guarantee you this morning will be beautiful, but you can know for sure there will be a hole or two out there waiting for you. It may even seem with every step forward you take you fall into that hole with Otis. This is not a peaceful situation to find yourself in.

As I See it, We Have Some Choices, and They Are:

- We can stay in that hole.

- We can cry and scream and even curse the hole for being there.

- We can climb out of that hole defeated and just forget our dream.

- We can pretend it didn't hurt as we limp on down the road.

- We can crawl out and retire--just live a remote life, free from others.

- We can, with God's help, climb out, dust ourselves off and be there to help others when they fall down.

How to Get Out of Holes of Anger and Resentment.

Often someone asks me to write about how to get out of a deep hole of anger or resentment or an unforgiving spirit. They have no peace. They are tired of screaming and yelling at the circumstances and the people responsible for the hole they are in. I've watched folks crawl in and out of holes for a heap of years. I have come to this conclusion: there is a difference in how the Christian who is the real thing and the one who is a counterfeit (sometimes unknowingly) climb out of holes. I think it all goes back to His words, "My peace I give you."

Oswald Chambers in his devotion book, "My Utmost for His Highest", says: "A real Christian sees everything he is dumped down in as the means of securing the knowledge of Jesus Christ." That is the beginning of our personal peace.

Wave This Banner as You Crawl Out of Your Hole.

I believe there are five little words in Philemon 3:10 (KJV) we could place on a banner and wave as we crawl out of the hole to continue on our way. They are simply, "That I may know Him." You see, peace is the outcome of the right knowing, loving relationship with our Lord.

Oh, I Forgot to Tell You the Name of the Movie. It is "Milo and Otis".

Are there any of you out there who feel the same way about Milo and Otis, the holes of life and the privilege of knowing Him as I do? If so, we need to get together. You bring the popcorn and I'll bring the Milk Duds.

CHAPTER NINE:

Let's Play Ball!

I never really had a choice but to love sports. God graced me with two sons and you know the rest of the story. First born played to win, second born played to have fun. Both reasons were okay. "You worked hard out there on the court or on the field," was always my response to games won or lost. Our first son still plays to win as the head high school coach for the Petal Panthers in Southern Mississippi. He sets his players up to be winners on the football field and in life. He works hard to do so and I still tell him after every win or loss, "You and your boys worked hard out there tonight. I love you." Sit back and enjoy my sports columns, even as I enjoyed writing them.

1. My Love Affair with Football
2. Is it an Ordinary Game of Baseball or of Life?
3. I Never Prayed to Win the Game
4. Don't Forget to Pack Enthusiasm on Your Road to the Final Four
5. What Position do You Want to Play?

MY LOVE AFFAIR WITH FOOTBALL

Every newspaper I open reminds me it's coming. Even magazines are featuring the beginning of another season. What's just around the corner? Football! Ladies, I have a confession to make. I have had a love affair with football for as long as I can remember.

MY FAVORITE FOOTBALL STORY

My favorite football story goes back to when we lived near Oxford, Mississippi in the '60's and "you know who" was the quarterback…it wasn't Payton or Eli. It was Archie Manning, their father. Our younger son was four. (He is now 41 or 42…can never remember how old my sons are.)

He and a group of future All-Americans were playing football in our backyard in Pontotoc, Mississippi. Even then, our seven-year-old son played coach as he yelled at the other players. (This one, who is somewhere around 45, is still yelling at his real players as he continues to coach.)

Looking out the back window I saw younger son, Stan, taking off his helmet and throwing it down as he started running toward the house. He was fighting mad. When I calmed him down to ask what was wrong he cried, "Steve won't let me be Archie Manning. I'm not 'gonna' ever play football with him again."

As a young mother I knew it was okay for my children to pretend to be someone else. Yet, I know folks who always want to be someone else. It is especially disturbing to see this in so many of our youth today. I wonder if we have failed to teach them to feel good about their God-given individuality … warts and all.

GO FIND A CHILD

May I suggest a beginning? Go find your child or your grandchild or just any child and say, "I like you." Don't say love. Say like. They need to be liked by you. May I ask you a question? When is the last time you complimented a child in your life?

Looking back over a lifetime of teaching, I have one hope. It is simple. I hope my many students can say of me, "Mrs. Buckley thought I "wuz" smarter than I "wuz," so I "wuz."

Come to think about it, over my many years of writing for this paper, I thank you for encouraging an unknown, unlearned, insecure beginning writer as she shared her life with you. Thank you for the many contacts leading me to believe I "wuz" smarter than I "wuz", so I "wuz."

SHARE OUR SECRET

Don't forget to share this secret with someone this coming week. By words or by deeds let just one person know you like them. Better still, find a child or a young person and whisper it in their ear instead of yelling at them about messing up. On the other hand, yelling is good when watching your favorite high school, college or pro football team playing hard. Can't wait for the season to open.

Is it an Ordinary Game of Baseball or of Life?

"Do you have an addiction?"

"Me ... an addiction? Don't be ridiculous!"

We know other folks have addictions. We may all hide a bad habit or two, but certainly not an addiction.

What does an addiction owner look like?

If you turn on your television any given weekend you can see as any as 90,000 addicts screaming or booing or even fighting. They are called fans. But in reality they could be folks with addictions to any sport. Football. Baseball. Basketball.

Today I pick baseball. Do you, as a fan, ever pay close attention to baseball announcers as well as the players, coaches and fans?

I realize they are announcing a baseball game, but what they really are doing is talking about life. Let me share with you what I heard from an announcer recently. Hopefully, it will cause you to pause and ponder the words of the game as well as the plays.

See if you agree. First comment:

"He can't find the plate."

I know the feeling, don't you? And I'm not even a pitcher. How many times have you simply not been able to find the plate no matter how hard you try? You miss the strike zone in every relationship, in every situation, with every effort. Those dreaded words echo in our minds and hearts ..."You're out!"

Back to the baseball chatter:

"He just hit the warning track."

I happen to believe, as we hit the warning track of life, our faith becomes personal. At this point, our Heavenly Father will protect us from head-on collisions in life if we have invited Him to play the game with us.

OUR ANNOUNCER IS BEAMING IN AGAIN GIVING INFORMATION ABOUT A CERTAIN PLAYER:

"He holds the bag at first base."

Only first base? Have you ever felt you have been holding the bag at first, second and third base forever? You may even be lost in the lonely outfield. As we hold on to our bases everyone is telling us what to do and when to do it. I know there is a squeeze play in baseball. There are also squeeze plays in life. In fact, sometimes I feel like I have been squeezed out. Do you? This is when I am very careful to pay attention to only God's voice.

It's the ninth inning and we hear:

"THAT WAS HIS TWENTIETH ERROR OF THE YEAR."

Only twenty? I must have made twenty just today. At this point frustration could topple us over and fling us down. Yet, it's okay. As we experience true frustration, we usually come away down and defeated. That is then we get in the position to listen to God.

As the game progresses you may think, "I'm not ready or sufficient for this. It's definitely not a fun experience."

When these thoughts enter your mind, it is a sign you have come to the realization your sufficiency is of God and in Him alone. It is by His rules you succeed in this game.

My relationship with God is the only addiction I want and need when I hear the words, "Play Ball! Batter Up!"

I Never Prayed to Win the Game

The phone rang. It was a simple request, "Will you speak to our Fellowship of Christian Athletes?"

Because I liked this high school cheerleader, I quickly said, "Yes. I'd be glad to do that for you."

Time to Panic

Then I panicked! Let me give you the complete picture of this long-ago conversation. I was fiftyish and fattish with varicose veins and gray hair. My only claim to being an athlete was that I was the jack champion at Pendorf School in Laurel back in the '50s … or was in the '40s?

What to do? I began that night of sharing with my only personal sports story. It goes like this:

Don't Dare Do It

When my older son was a senior in high school we traveled all across South Mississippi playing football using the Notre Dame Box where there is no quarterback. At one strategic game I heard my name being called, "Billie, are you sure I can't pray to win this game?"

Eddie was in my young couples' Bible study class. On the previous Sunday I told them I had never prayed to win a game. Some twenty years later I still have never done so.

I answered back, "No, Eddie. Don't pray to win this game."

Time to Laugh

Later, it was fourth down with two yards to go on their ten yard line when he loudly called out, "Billie, can I pray to make a first down?

"No, Eddie. Don't pray to make a first down."

We did win the game. Afterwards as we were hugging all those dirty, sweaty boys, Eddie came up with a big smile.

"Eddie, you didn't?'

"Oh, no…I didn't pray to win the game, but I did pray for the other team to lose."

May I suggest to you there is more to prayer than praying to win? You may want to ask if you don't pray to win, can you pray?

HOW TO PRAY

Every day from September 1 to November 28 in 1980, I wrote a special prayer for our son's football team. I did this believing it would make a difference in the lives of the players and coaches on that team and not on the score. By the way, most all those young coaches were in the class I taught at our church in Natchez.

One example was written the first of November. I wrote: "We lost in a bad, unfair way. Father, it is hard to see Your design in losing. But I read in John 8:36 (KJV), 'Ye shall be free indeed.'"

These words led me to pray, "Help our sons to be free from the resentment of the loss Friday night and free from personal failures. They have been designed with a great capacity for You, Lord. Fill this capacity with Yourself. Amen."

A HAPPY ENDING

Oh, I almost forgot to tell you I entitled my prayer gift to my son, "A Season of Joy."

His team became known as the 1980 Big Eight Championship Team and were voted the Number One High School Football Team in the state of Mississippi. He no long plays football. He now coaches football. You will hear me screaming on any given Friday night this fall, "Go Petal Panthers."

Don't Forget to Pack Enthusiasm on Your Road to the Final Four

"Take an educated guess." When I taught school, that's what I repeatedly told my sixth graders. Today I want you to take an educated guess. Just guess what My Favorite Preacher and I have been doing for weeks.

I'll give you a clue. One of my favorite movies is "Hoosiers." When I'm having a downer day or am unmotivated, all I need to do is sit quietly, watch this movie and have myself a good "cure."

You guessed it. We have been watching basketball games and having a great time on the Road to the Final Four. I must confess "coach watching" is almost as much fun as watching the game being played.

The Lost Emotion

One word best describes the beginning of each game…enthusiasm. We live in such a sophisticated, tired world. Right? At times, even church folks seem to have lost their lively enthusiasm. Many marriages or family relationships are void of this particular emotion. What about our jobs? Some feel work was and is just a bad joke and definitely nothing to be upbeat about. (Teachers can easily fall into this trap.)

Got to Get on the Right Road

Now if you must mourn this lack of enthusiasm, then mourn for a season. Appoint a day of mourning. Put on sackcloth and ashes and have at it. Let me warn you about this mourning party. You won't attract many participants for long; but if you hope to draw a crowd, muster up some enthusiasm.

Some of you are women with a triple workload of motherhood, homemaking and employment. I realize you may not have a passion for work. You simply work for family preservation and survival. Let me assure you, I'm not writing about something I have read. I juggled those three balls for 32 years.

Dads, I invite you to pull up a chair and listen. In order for your family to survive you have to be a survivor. How can you be a worthy worker (that's biblical) and keep a pleasant personality (that's also biblical) at the same time? Can it be done?

I think it can, if you get on the right road. Let's put it this way … the Final Four objectives in your life of responsibilities should be the following: a sense of fun, a sense of satisfaction, a sense of creativity, and a sense of productivity. Let's get on these roads one at a time.

ROAD TO FUN

Learn to flow, stay loose and laugh out loud. Remember there are ways you should never grow up. This is one of them. You don't have to appoint a Fun Committee, but it might help. You probably know some folks who definitely cannot be chairman of that committee. Could you? Don't forget the Bible says a merry heart is good medicine all the way through its pages.

THE ROAD TO SATISFACTION

Take pride in what you do. Don't let our society's stilted sense of values rob you of your sense of satisfaction as you value what God values. Any worthy work can be gratifying if you honestly do your dead-level best and enjoy doing it with enthusiasm. The Word reminds us, "Whatsoever your hands find to do, do it with all your might."

ROAD TO CREATIVITY

Now being creative does not mean you have to paint a picture or write an original song. It may mean you can think of a new way to teach an old truth, or resolve a problem, or just involve more folks in the process of becoming enthusiastic. Don't forget to let God be as creative in other people as He is in you.

ROAD TO PRODUCTIVITY

Once I got a heart-warming letter from a young man who had his first job in a church as a youth director. He wrote, "It is amazing to me how few people actually use their brains. I have found you can be productive if you put your mind and efforts into working out your problems. I further think the solution could be quite simple if you included God. Thank you for reminding me He is still around."

IT'S OKAY TO BE PROUD

Can you keep a secret? Believe it or not, our #1 Son does not always read this column. So if you don't tell, maybe I can sneak something by him. I am proud to have a son who has returned to the sidelines as a coach. If you call on Friday night, just leave a message. We won't be home. We will be back in the stands yelling with enthusiasm, "Go Panthers!"

What Position Do You Want To Play?

This column has to be about basketball. This is March Madness Month. There's no telling how many college basketball games My Favorite Preacher and I have watched, nor how many more we will watch. (The most fun was seeing USM win its last game real and in person.)

I Want to be the Point Guard

I've even decided what position I want to play. The decision was made while watching the LSU women's team. I want to be the point guard. Forgetting what it was called made no difference. I knew the position was for me as a writer.

Okay, let me assist you in making some smart decisions. Through this column, I'm passing the ball to you.

First Passed Ball

The first pass is to parents. Thumbing through a magazine, I read about the bully's new playground. Through 32 years of teaching, many bullies showed up in my classroom. These I could control. Now they have invaded our homes through the World Wide Web. The internet is the new playground.

The story began with the tragic result of a 13-year-old committing suicide because of the power of words written by on-line bullies. Parents, make it your business to know what is going on in your child's life, especially if there is a computer in his/her room.

Educate them. Educate school officials. Educate youth leaders.

Websites were given: cyberbulling.org; i-safe.org; mindon.com.

This week I have passed the ball to a great youth director, to the parents of my five grandchildren and to you. Pass it on. Stop the internet bullying.

Second Passed Ball

The second pass is to book lovers. First, I need to find our two grown sons and ask their forgiveness for not encouraging them to watch the television program "Mister Roger's Neighborhood." when they were little. In this program Mr. Rogers, without mentioning God, reflected the spiritual values he held dear.

He once told the author of this book, May Hollingsworth, "I'm convinced the space between the television and the viewer is holy ground. This is made possible when it is translated by the Holy Spirit to meet the needs of the person watching."

If I can't find our two sons today, I'll just buy them each this book, "The Simple Faith of Mr. Rogers" and pass it on to them.

CHAPTER TEN:

Listening to Friends and Readers

To all who have encouraged me over the years as a writer since 1986, I say, "Thank you for putting some good on my life through your letters and emails and friendly visits where we just met up with each other. My purpose was always to help my readers see the good all around them. The ideas did not come from being locked in an Ivory Tower and meditating. They came form noisy ballgames; in a busy classroom; cleaning my house, or at 4:30 on many a cold, dark morning squeezing in time to write before leaving for school. To those who looked and could find no good I thank you for not writing, 'That's bad.'" In this last chapter my hope for you is you will find a keeping thought or two to keep on keeping on.

1. Thank You for Friends
2. It Pays To Team Up With Others
3. Sharing Our Needs
4. The First Shall Be Last

THANK YOU FOR FRIENDS

Do you remember I once told you that I was "sixtyish" and "fattish?" It is getting close to that time in my life when I have to change one of those descriptive words, and it's not "fattish." Believe me; I will never be "thinnish!"I can't bring myself to say it, but maybe I can write it. I will be 70 this coming year … 2009. There. I've admitted it. Even so, it's still painful.

THIS I REMEMBER

I remember, when I was still young, and turned fifty. About thirty old friends came one weekend. They came bearing, among other things, black balloons and other over-the-hill reminders.

These special friends were part of a young couple's class I had taught for over seven years in our previous church. We laughed and cried and worshipped and ate together. Oh, how we did eat together!

There's a popular song that says, "People who need people are the luckiest people in the world." That qualifies me as being lucky. I'm not ashamed to say to my friends, "I need you."

I NEED YOU

To the group of kids I taught, I can honestly say, "I needed you to keep me young; to challenge my mind, my patience and my sanity at times."

To the people in my church I say, "I need you to sing along with me. By myself I sound puny and weak. But when you and I blend our voices together, I can sing with gusto and praise to the One who is worthy of our worship."

To my lasting friends I can say, "I need the breathing room you always know when to give me. I need to feel the dignity of your friendship and to share our failures as well as our successes."

Do you have a friendship that is in the Intensive Care Unit? If so, let me make a few suggestions that might lead to a deeper understanding of friendship and to a full recovery.

Recipe for Friendships

- Don't expect too much from a friend … at times both of you need to be lonely.

- If you are a friend, you can brag about your friend doing something better than you can. You can inflate his busted balloon without being jealous.

- Know that friendship will cost you. It takes time and effort and understanding to be a friend.

- Being comfortable around people is a true sign of healthy friendships. Silence is never awkward.

- Feeling safe with a person is another mark of friendship.

- Separation doesn't end a friendship if it's not centered on competing against each other and impressing each other.

- Genuine friends are those we learn from, are encouraged by and never forget.

- I don't have to agree with you to be your friend. I do owe you my forgiveness when needed. You owe me the same when needed.

My Best Friend

I have only one friend who meets all these qualifications. I learned a song about Him when I was a little girl. It goes like this:

My best friend is Jesus. Love Him. Love Him.

My best friend is Jesus. Serve Him. Serve Him.

My best friend is Jesus. Thank Him. Thank Him.

With this song ringing in my mind, surely I must pray, "Thank you for friends, and thank you for letting me be grow older and hopefully wiser. May I grow old loving You, serving You and thanking You. Amen … so be it."

IT PAYS TO TEAM UP WITH OTHERS

Everybody's doing it…well, not everybody but a lot of folks in Mississippi are doing it. They are teaming up with somebody to write a book. Today I've decided to team up with other writers for this meandering.

Let's be honest, our minds embrace what we are passionate about and what we live for. In Mississippi we are passionate about eating. I am positive some of you are like me, no matter where you live. When it comes to food preparation, you want to simplify the process. Starting from scratch is not on our agenda. With this in mind, I have invited some five year olds to team up with me and share their simple recipes with you. Here are four of my favorites:

Con Pie: Get some cons. Put the cons on a piecrust. Put it in the stove. Cook the pie for three minutes. Take it out, put it on a plate and eat it until it is all gone.

Cheese Cake: Buy a box with cheesecake mix on it. Mix it up. Pour it in the piecrust. Put it in the oven. Hide the box.

Pizza: Call Pizza Hut. Send Daddy to the store. (That has got to be my favorite recipe.)

French Fries: Cut up the potatoes. Put the potatoes in a skillet. Cook for six hours. Eat with ketchup. Be careful. They are so hot.

I also invited my Creative Writing Class to share some of their comfort food experiences from their growing up days. My hope is these stories will revive some of your long ago family memories.

Vivian Coats: Crispy fat and crunchy lean. Cracklings hot from a huge black wash pot. Daddy butchered hogs on the first cold days in late fall. These delicious morsels were mostly used to make crackling cornbread, but they were just as good by themselves. There must have been 100 grams of fat in a small handful. Who was counting? Not me.

Debbie Little: Growing up Italian has its advantages. Sunday mornings were filled with the aroma of simmering spaghetti sauce prepared by my mother. Every week we were delighted with lasagna, manicotti, ravioli and the like. Frequently I attempt to duplicate my mother's wonderful recipes, but it's not the same. Just maybe I don't have as much Italian in me as my Mother did.

Russlyn Carter: The making of gumbo was a big production for my mother: peeling, chopping, stirring to the right consistency and color. The smell reminded us company was coming and added to the excitement. What great gumbo memories are triggered for me by these long ago thoughts of my big, noisy family.

Roblyn R. Schwartz: My grandmother, Bessie Hill, knew how to cook. Nana could mix ordinary ingredients and produce mouth-watering results. Perched on my red metal folding stool, I watched as she created my favorite dessert, banana pudding. With the spoon clinking against the double boiler, Nana stirred sugar, flour, milk and eggs to send my taste buds watering. Next the Pyrex dish was lined with vanilla wafers and layered with ripe bananas and the warm creamy pudding. The best part was licking the spoon and cleaning out the large double boiler.

Tommy Mangum: My memory takes me back to childhood when cotton was cultivated by mule. It was a time when the Sunday chicken for dinner was a rooster walking around the chicken yard on Saturday morning. It was time when having bacon or ham on the breakfast table meant dressing the sacrificial pig. This ritual took place every November when the weather turned cold. These memories are etched in my mind as clearly as a painted mural on a giant plastered wall.

Do you know the greatest recipe book ever written was the Bible? This is because nothing in human experience is ever left out of the Bible. All the ingredients are there. If you are a Christian, you too must team up with someone; that someone is the Holy Spirit living in you. Just this morning, I found a perfect recipe for our hectic days: "My presence shall go with you, and I will give you rest." Exodus 33:14 (KJV)

My hope is you will have a restful time teaming up with His presence. "Bon Appetite"

SHARING OUR NEEDS

I got mail for over 20 years in P.O. Box 1133 Petal, MS, 39465 or on ggbb@comcast.net.

One letter read: "Surely God led you to write your Saturday article just for me. His timing was perfect, and I stand amazed. By now you must know I am hemmed in, boxed up, and at a dead end because of a major problem. Please include me in your prayers."

The all-time favorite column ... the column more folks pull from their purse, yellow and worn out asked the question, "Are you a clutternite?" I wrote it was okay to have countless pictures of family, friends, books, and old shoes scattered about. It was okay to take time to dream and swing and to clutter your life up with folks who are hurting.

ENCOURAGEMENT FROM READERS TO KEEP ON

God moved and readers wrote. "There is so much horror in the paper, but your articles lift my spirits and give me hope. Thanks for sharing your self and your family. It is helpful to me to see God's love through ordinary families. Take the time to continue to write. God will send the ideas."

Others wrote."It is raining this morning. When I went to get the paper, you visited me over a cup of coffee. You really hit the spot today. How hard it is to see color in my world and not to worry. Thanks to your columns, I have a real friend."

God led her to write, "I have tried for several weeks to think of the right words to write to you because of the special way you write about your family in your column. I really felt God was leading me to write. Then God gave me the words through your column. Thank you for the pearls you have dropped into my life."

Another letter addressed to me read, "We own a country store. The daily routine of life sometimes gets depressing, even at Christmas time. Your article always lifts me up. Some of my favorites are on the file cabinet in our store. I reread them often. I've noticed other people do so, too. If you're ever on Highway 84, drop in and have a cup of coffee with us."

ENCOURAGEMENT FROM A GOOD FRIEND

Many times this friend, Nova, has interrupted my life with laughter and friendship. You will find her on my refrigerator door. A button holds her there and also holds her to my heart. It reads, "You have touched me and I have grown." She may live far away, yet I know she is always available to understand, to encourage, or to listen.

Hopefully, my readers will always feel that way about my writing. Through oneness with my Father's mind, motive of love, and movement I will continue to write. And the words I write will touch others, and they will grow.

This was my first column ever written for the Hattiesburg American and it is the last one written for this my legacy book. Enjoy.

Anybody Tired or Lonely or Running out of Cope?

Have you ever wanted to grab the controls of your life (if you could find them) and "fast forward" your struggles, "rewind" your triumphs, "pause" in your happiness, "erase" your mistakes, or just push the "off" button for a few days?

If so, we are related. May I share with you some ordinary daily experiences in hope that this honesty will encourage you to push the "play" button and enjoy life!

Have you lost the controls?

Did I hear you say that you too have lost the controls of your life, or did you say that you have so much to do that there's not time to look for them? No, that's not your problem. You have nothing but empty hours, and somehow you yourself are lost in your uselessness. Either way, there is a problem.

Normally, when I lose something it's because there's too much clutter. Could there just possibly be **too** much clutter in our lives? Are you interested in how to get rid of the clutter and simplify your life so that you can at least locate the controls?

Where is the first place to look?

The first place you may need to look is in someone's hands -- your boss, your wife, your husband, your older parents, your children, even your friends. If you are an adult, none of these people should be in control of your life. You are responsible for pushing those buttons that produce happiness and pain in your own life.

Once you locate the controls, remove all but one butt**on**. That's the button that brings your life into focus with one word, probably the most important word in the English language, relationships. Until I understood this, my life was always out of balance and needing to be focused.

Where was my broken table?

Once I had a cute little table with two good legs and one cracked leg. My sons, Steve and Stan, would come in and plop their books on the table every day. Every day it would fall. One day I came home from teaching school and my cute little table was gone. To this day, nobody knows what happened to that table, but I do know that it was useless. It was useless because it was built to stand on three legs and only two were working. That table was made to be balanced.

What do we need to be balanced?

You and I are made to be balanced with three right relationships - a right relationship of oneness with ourselves, with others and with *God*. If that oneness relationship is not right, your life may look good like my table did, but it's as useless as was my table. I think that's what Christ meant in Matthew 22:37-40 (KJV). Look it up and see what you think. From my heart to your heart.

Thank you for strolling with me through my life. I hope you too have taken time to dream and swing. Let's not to forget invite a busy person to come on in and sit a spell with us and Our Lord.

Billie Buckley … speaker, writer and teacher will tell you the only excuse for her life is her relationship with Jesus Christ. Her formal teaching experiences include 32 years of teaching in the classroom. She is retired from school teaching but continues to teach in churches and to ladies involved in the Christian Women's Job Core Ministry in two locations.

Billie has written a column for the Hattiesburg American newspaper for the past twenty years. From her original columns a short booklet was published. She has also written for denominational magazines and papers. Her latest denominational work was a three-month study on the book of Jeremiah for the Sunday school lesson review for the Mississippi Baptist Record. She now serves on the Advisory Committee for this paper. For years she has taught a writing class where all work was edited by her, and some of the class writing has been self published.

She is also involved with working for 225 children in Honduras through Baptist Dental and Medical Missions Inc. This work mainly involves raising funds for the uniforms and the work of the Awana program in the Good Shepherd School. Her influence is also felt through working on the Personnel Committee for selecting missionaries for this program.

As a speaker she moves from churches to clubs to restaurants to schools. Billie crosses denominational lines and age differential, taking God's word into our lives with humor and openness.

Family is front and center in her life. This includes the minister to whom she has been married for 50 years. After retiring he served as an interim pastor for seven years and is now, in the year 2009, pastor of the Sunrise Baptist Church just two miles from their home.

She has five grandchildren, and two daughters-in-law who are her heroes. Son Number One is owner of Bucko's Cleaners in Petal and the head football coach at Petal High School in Petal, Miss. Son Number Two is the senior pastor of First Baptist Church in Jackson, Miss.

Putting good on others' lives by bearing fruit is the over-all purpose of her life as she seeks to be one with God's mind, motives and movement to bring His children home.

Breinigsville, PA USA
15 December 2009
229263BV00002B/3/P